Body *Sense*

Revolutionize Your Riding
with the Alexander Technique

Sally A. Tottle

Body *Sense*

Revolutionize Your Riding
with the Alexander Technique

by **Sally A. Tottle**

Foreword by Sally Swift

Trafalgar Square Publishing
North Pomfret, Vermont

First published in 1998 by
Trafalgar Square Publishing
North Pomfret, Vermont 05053

Disclaimer of Liability:
The author and publisher shall have neither liability nor responsibility to any person or entity with respect to any loss or damage caused or alleged to be caused directly or indirectly by the information contained in this book. While the book is as accurate as the author can make it, there may be errors, omissions, and inaccuracies.

Library of Congress Cataloging-in-Publication Data
Tottle, Sally A.
BodySense : revolutionize your riding with the Alexander Technique /
by Sally A. Tottle ; foreword by Sally Swift.
cm.
Includes bibliographical references (p.   ) and index.
ISBN 1-57076-048-9
Horsemanship. 2. Alexander technique.   I. Title.
SF309.T68   1998
798.2'3—dc21   98-3140
                                                                              CIP

Cover and book design by Edith Crocker
Typeface: Bembo 11.5/14

Printed in Canada
10 9 8 7 6 5 4 3 2 1

ACKNOWLEDGMENTS

"BODYSENSE" ORIGINALLY STARTED as a joint project with Michael Masterman, Member, Society of Teachers of the Alexander Technique (MSTAT). I owe him a great deal of thanks for co-writing the synopsis and some of the chapters before he decided to change direction. Minette Rice-Edwards has spent many hours with me, burning the midnight oil and prompting me with thought-provoking questions and careful editing. Her undaunting encouragement and cajoling humour have kept me on track. I am eternally grateful to Daniel Pevsner for writing the preface, and for his awe-inspiring knowledge. His consistent assurance and help in clarifying ideas has meant a great deal to me. Sally Swift for graciously agreeing to write a foreword. Peter and Stella Clifford, have given generously of their time and advice. Laura Fry for her kind words. Caroline Robbins, my publisher, who is already known for publishing innovative books on riding and horses. Her expertise on making such books a joy to read is cherished. Martha Cook, also from Trafalgar Square, has diligently helped with editing and layout. Carol Trippel, who spent time copyediting and styling the manuscript. Walter Carrington has given freely of his advice and knowledge, in particular with page 59. Dr. Kathryn Ballard gave valuable help with physiology. Many thanks to Karen Jones, who has diligently typed the manuscript and must be one of the few people in the world who can decipher my handwriting. Christopher Taylor's unwavering support, intuition and wisdom have inspired me to reach the end.

Christopher Smart has produced some wonderful photographs and I would like to acknowledge him for his talent and attention to detail. Sebastian Rice-Edwards for his lively drawings. Alex Newcombe for her valued contribution. Colin, Julia, and Elisa Tully for their photos. Jo Taylor for her illustrations that depict movement so well. Mary Scott for the photo of Alexander reproduced by Allen Jones. Jan Farnes, cartoonist, has made humorous translations from the text. David Gorman allowed me to use his wonderful drawings from the "Body Moveable," for which I am most grateful. Harriet Harrison and Sara

Salmon were wonderful models and gave me the use of their house and facilities, which helped to make creative photographs. Thanks also to Sonya French and the photo location at Triggles House Arabian Stud.

Many thanks to Jacqui Stoddart for giving me the chance to write at her beautiful house in the Black Mountains. The Hayden Family also allowed me to use their idyllic farm where writing flowed more readily. Frank Harmer, ceramicist and writer, encouraged and advised me on how to break into the writing world. The late Douglas Bevan's enthusiasm inspired me. Alison Bridge of *Horse & Rider* magazine published my first articles. I would also like to thank Alison for her kind endorsement and Carl Hester for his support. I also want to thank all my teachers, friends, and pupils. In particular, Sue Adams-Wheeler, Terese Angwin, April Budgeon, Carol Broad, Nick Burton, Alison Brough, Robin Broadbank, Jeremy Chance, Kath Creemer, Di Freeman, Keith Davison, Lorna Fisher-Watkins, Lyn Gambles, Val Jones, Isabel Haskett, Rosie Humphries, Sue Kear, Caroline Langhorn, the late Diana Mason, Susie Neville-Parker, Marcy Pavord, Irina Jackson, Sylvia Philpin-Jones, Vivien and Hal Plews, Julie Reece, Fiona Renton, Claire Richardson, Jenny Sampson, Laween Street, Lin Smith, Eleanor Slater, and Karen Tibbetts.

To all the horses who have taught me so much especially Spartacus (Spooks), who still has a sense of humour after twenty years, and Ndaba and Divine. My parents who always encouraged me to realise my dreams, and last, but not least, my Aunt Marjorie Miller who took seriously the scribbling of an eight-year-old who was going to write a book about ponies. This is a somewhat different version!

Contents

FOREWORD

This wonderful book is easy to read, clear, concise, and well organized. Sally Tottle has a fund of information on how to use our bodies with harmony and ease resulting in vastly improved relationships with our horses.

The Alexander Technique is extraordinarily difficult to fully express in words as it is so dependent on the student learning through the touch and directives of the teacher's hands. Sally has done an exceptionally good job, but to receive the greatest impact from this book, it becomes essential that the student, of whatever level of riding expertise, receive first hand experience with a teacher of the Alexander Technique, and preferably one who understands horses and riding.

Even without the help of an Alexander teacher, this book will bring new insights on the importance of becoming aware of our habitual, often incorrect, ways of using our bodies. It teaches any rider how, almost invariably, improved awareness and body use will subtly and often dramatically improve horsemanship and life.

This book should be a "must" in any horseman's library. It will be just that for all my teachers and our students.

—Sally Swift, author of *Centered Riding*
1998

PREFACE

Horsemanship and the Alexander Technique

I began taking Alexander lessons about twelve years ago, because my back was in pain whenever I got on a horse, and because I was hoping to improve my riding position. The very first few lessons won me over completely. Everything was working well. The pain cleared, and I was changing shape quite dramatically. I was nearly ready to get bored with the whole thing when I began to realize the wider implications of the technique for me, as a professional, working with horses. I found a great resemblance between the ideals of good posture and locomotion, as applied to horses or to people. The concepts and the procedures involved in attaining these ideals were not dissimilar. This to me was of the utmost importance. It dawned on me that, by learning the technique, I might achieve some of the equestrian experience that was then to me unobtainable. By studying the technique, I was gaining a better view and understanding of horsemanship, and at the same time, my riding experience convinced me of the validity, and the soundness of the technique.

A further step in my development occurred some months later, when, in the Autumn of 1969, the Spanish Riding School of Vienna came to England. The school has been in existence for over 400 years and is today regarded as a custodian of the art of horsemanship. The kind of riding practised in the school is called dressage. This can mean simply the basic schooling that every riding horse has to undergo, irrespective of what his job in life is going to be, but at its advanced level, dressage consists of high-school figures and movements, which, in equine locomotion, are the equivalent of human ballet.

I had not seen the school perform live before, and the impact on me was quite staggering. The equestrian standard of the display was, of course, very high, and very satisfying, but what struck me in particular, was the superb *use*★ and posture of the riders. Although I was already

---

★ *Use* is a word that has an unusual and expanded meaning in the practice of the Alexander Technique. Its sense will become more clear as you read this book, but for now it is easiest to think of *use* as a combination of posture, coordination, and management of tension.

at the time developing a new awareness and appreciation of good *use*, and even though I was by then a fairly experienced riding teacher, it was not until this meeting with the Spanish School that I realized to what extent one could develop one's own good *use*, through correct riding. The riders before me were carrying themselves and acting as if they had all undergone thorough training in the technique. It then became obvious to me, that in order to become a really top class rider, one would have to develop qualities that would be instantly recognised and appreciated by an Alexander teacher. Later on, when I got to know the riders in person, I discovered that their training influenced not only their behaviour in the saddle, but also their general *use* in everyday life, which, indeed, I found to be excellent.

Experience shows that those who have had some Alexander training make very apt riding pupils, and that their progress is unusually quick. They, of course, start with some very great advantages, such as correct posture, independent use of limbs, a highly developed sense of balance, and very important, they pause to think before they act. On the other hand, riders who take up the technique always make a very significant improvement. For some, it may make all the difference as to whether they will ever become competent riders.

A good riding position offers the rider security and comfort in the saddle and enables him to guide, and control his horse with ease and efficiency. Equally important, a good riding position reduces to a minimum any discomfort that may be caused to the horse by the presence of weight on his back. An old definition of the rider's position describes it in the following words:

"The rider should sit as upright as possible, so that each part of his body rests on that which is immediately below it, and produces a direct vertical pressure, through the seat bones."

We all know, of course, how difficult it is to produce this position even when sitting in an ordinary chair. The rider, however, has to maintain this uprightness while sitting on a surface whose texture and movements vary from moment to moment, and which at times can be extremely uncomfortable. The horse's movement takes place, simultaneously, in both horizontal and vertical directions. At times the horse may also move on a curve or even sideways. All this action has to be absorbed by the rider, while keeping upright, in a position that is always vertical to the ground. This calls for a very high degree of firm suppleness. The rider's body must acquire the properties of flexible steel, which can blend and absorb pressure, while retaining its resilience and which can always recapture its original shape.

Of particular interest to the Alexander minded person, is the rider's ability to influence and control the horse through the appropriate use of his own back. This action which riders describe as "bracing the back," is brought about when the rider modifies the texture of his spine. He does so by altering the amount of stretch and tension that runs through the spine, and by giving the spine a particular direction. The bracing of the back is sometimes accompanied by a subtle displacement of the rider's sense of gravity. All these adjustments must take place within the outline of the position, and must not be seen from the outside. The influence of the rider's back on the horse is both very powerful, and very delicate. When it is synchronized with the legs and hands, it is capable of producing a countless number of directional combinations. When the rider braces his back, he is in fact using his spine as a working tool, as another limb, which can be activated or adjusted at will. This way of employing the spine is, I believe, unique to riders. While all physical activity requires the use of one's back, it is only in riding that the spine is brought into action in such a precise and deliberate manner.

The training of the rider consists of a series of controlled sensory experiences, all calling on the rider to continually re-adjust himself in order to blend with the horse's movement, while maintaining a correct position. The instructor, by using variations of gait, speed, and direction, is constantly exposing his pupil to different situations in which his balance and suppleness are newly tested.

Ultimately, horse and rider reach a state of complete unity where their separate bodies seem to have merged together, and to be acting as one. This harmony between horse and rider can be so complete that just a thought on the part of the rider is enough to trigger a response in the horse. This, of course, would make sense to an Alexander person. We have all experienced this kind of closeness with a teacher, or with a pupil. Also we know only too well how a thought, or its *inhibition*, can affect a body's reactions.

"Preventing the wrong" is an important teaching concept, which applies equally to the technique and to horsemanship. What it really tells us, is that a living body cannot be forced to act in a particular manner; at the most it can be coaxed into doing so. The main teaching of a subject that requires *sensory appreciation* is based on the prevention of wrong *use* and on the *inhibition* of undesirable responses. This is not to say that there is no room for positive, active teaching. Explanation, advice, a guiding touch, a stimulus are all of immense value. Yet none of these can substitute for the thing that really matters, that is the feel of what is correct. The teacher is inherently limited, in that he is unable to convey to the pupil what the "correct" actually feels like; all he can do is guide the pupil there and point it out to him, when he, the pupil has arrived. It is a primary quality in a teacher to be able to recognise immediately that his pupil is doing the right thing. The riding teacher must also be able to know from the look of things what they feel like, and from the feel of things, what they look like. In riding, the teacher tries, on the one hand to stop every bit of *misuse* at the merest hint of its appearance, and on the other to guide the rider in his search for fresh directions. Eventually the rider hits on just the right combination of balance, strength, and flexibility that is required in the given situation. The first to acknowledge the rider's changed *use* and improved application will be the horse, who will then do, instantly, what was expected of him all the time, and for which the rider, until then, had to struggle. In riding, the best teachers are the horses because they instinctively know the good from the bad.

In schooling horses, much the same process takes place. While we cannot force the horse to act in a certain manner, we can make the existing pattern of its behaviour somewhat unattractive to it, and thereby encourage it to seek a better alternative. By combining the action of our back, legs and hands, or in other words by applying our aids, we help the horse to channel its energies in a better direction; when the horse finally gets it right, we instantly reward it. The kind of movement and carriage we ask the horse to adopt comes easily enough to it, when it is free, and out on its own. What is so difficult for the horse is to recapture its natural style and ability under the weight of the rider. Once the horse discovers the means of achieving this, it starts doing so of its own accord, because, of course, it is so much more comfortable. Until the horse chooses to put itself in what we regard as the desired position, that is the framework which encourages efficiency and ease, and until the horse is doing so by giving itself correct muscular directions while inhibiting the wrong ones, its training is not complete.

An Alexander person, observing a well-schooled horse, will soon discern certain similar attitudes in the way the animal moves and carries itself. The horse's head rotates forward and up at a point just behind the ears, while the lower jaw softens. His neck too, stretches forward and up, into a slight arch, as the back lengthens and widens. The horse's limb action appears to originate in its back, which indeed is the center of motion. Breathing is regular, and the back is smoothly pulsating all the time, imparting grace and elasticity to the movement. The expression on the face of the horse is that of great contentment. When we see this sight which is truly unforgettable, let us pause and reflect. The horse has given us pleasure and service throughout the ages. Yet all the while it was bringing us an even greater gift; a gift of life; the lesson of good *use*. It was all there, right in front of us. All that was missing was a genius of the caliber of Mr. Alexander, to put two and two together.

—F.M. Alexander Memorial Lecture 1980 by Daniel Pevsner, Fellow of the British Horse Society, Member of the Society of Teachers of the Alexander Technique, and Pupil of the Spanish Riding School

A Few Words about BodySense

It gives me much pleasure to be asked to preface and recommend Sally Tottle's timely book. We live in an age where horse-riding as a leisure activity has expanded beyond all recognition. At the same time there is a strong craving among riders to rediscover the skills and the beauty of the art of classical horsemanship. For most riders this would have remained a dream because of the length of time, cost and inaccessibility of suitable training establishments and because of the general shortage of good instruction. It is only in recent times that we have discovered how much can be gained by employing modern mind-body techniques to supplement and enhance traditional training methods, thus enabling the amateur rider to reach new levels of proficiency and satisfaction. In my experience the Alexander Technique is perhaps the best technique for this purpose.

It is notoriously difficult to convey Alexander's work in words — it is so dependent on real sensory experience that words cannot describe it. Sally Tottle has made a wonderful attempt at this; her writing is based on her own experiences as a teacher of the Alexander Technique and as a rider. Most importantly, she has tested and proven the effectiveness and the usefulness of Alexander's work through her numerous "BodySense" workshops.

—Daniel Pevsner, 1997

INTRODUCTION

"YOU WILL RIDE IN THE SAME MANNER AS YOU WALK" a wise riding instructor once told me. Unfortunately, I never understood the true meaning of those words until years later when Candida Denison, a musician friend, introduced me to the Alexander Technique. At the time, I was still recovering from a riding accident in which I had severely compressed two vertebrae, and seemed to be getting worse rather than better despite a two year time lapse. I could only ride or walk for a very short time and a full-time job was out of the question.

An orthopedic surgeon had recommended a bone fusion operation, but even then the chances of success were questionable. Before I resorted to the operation I decided to explore other avenues.

I shall never forget my first Alexander lesson. "Although you've been injured, the way you are standing, sitting, and walking is actually exacerbating your pain" my teacher explained. With the subtle use of her hands around my head and neck, she began to alter my coordination. Aided by a mirror, she showed me how I was putting even more pressure on my damaged spine by tipping my pelvis forward, which made the muscles around my injury contract and compress even more.

As my teacher brought about a change in the way I was standing, it felt strange and unfamiliar, but the pain began to diminish. By the end of the session, I felt as if a huge weight had been lifted from my back. After years of pain, it was such a relief. Here was a way of moving that could not only help my injury but could teach me how to use my body so that I could ride again.

Inspired, I returned to Somerset where I located Irina Jackson, Member, Society of Teachers of the Alexander Technique (MSTAT). Not only was she a talented teacher who herself had experienced back pain, she also understood my longing to ride seriously again.

At that time I was making ceramic sculptures and she realised that this was hampering my recovery. After a couple of months she made me an offer: if I stopped my ceramics for a time she would take me to Hertfordshire to visit Daniel Pevsner (Alexander Teacher, ex-pupil of the Spanish Riding School, and Fellow of the British Horse Society (F.B.H.S.). I agreed and arrangements were made for me to have both an Alexander and a riding session.

At that time I could only sit on a horse for ten minutes at the most. Danny explained that if I rode well, riding would help strengthen my back. Bad riding was probably the most harmful thing I could do for it. Although I had been longed as a child, the longe lesson I received from Danny was a totally new experience. Here was someone who knew how to instruct me to use my body in a way that put less strain on my back.

By applying what I had learned in my lessons with Irina, I was able to direct and coordinate myself without hurting! A new door had opened and at last my chances of riding seriously looked as if they could become reality. I was so impressed by this "new way of riding" that I continued to make regular visits to Danny and have trained with him ever since.

This book evolved from constant requests for further reading on riding and the Alexander Technique. I do hope you enjoy it and find it thought-provoking enough to try a lesson.

You will notice that the rider is referred to as "she" and the horse as "he." I'm not sexist but it does make for smoother reading!

Cloud Nine, Goodrich, England
August 1997

A Note to the Reader

The author has provided a glossary for her readers. The words defined in the glossary appear throughout the book in *italicised* type as an indication to the reader that they may refer to page 93 at the rear of the book for term definitions.

I

What is BodySense?

The BodySense Course

*"The impression of harmony
is much more important than the intricacy
of step and figures."* –Udo Bürger[1]

When we see a horse and rider performing really well together, it can be a totally captivating and inspiring experience. The horse moves easily and freely, the rider sits effortlessly poised while the application of her aids is almost imperceptible. Horse and rider blend together so completely that it becomes impossible to distinguish which one is guiding the other (figure 1.1).

Before a rider can fully learn the skill of riding a horse, she needs a foundation in good balance and body control. The Alexander Technique can help riders to find the elegance and poise they have admired in others that allow horse and rider to move as one. Once learned this will help to develop the suppleness, coordination, correct muscle tone, stability, and sensitivity that are the foundations for good riding.

Unfortunately, there are very few trainers who can teach balance and body control, and not many who even realise how important it is to establish these qualities in the rider before the horse can be correctly trained. The majority of instruction available is limited because it fails to address these basic preconditions.

In 1988 I completed my three-year Alexander Teacher training. During the course, I realised that all riders, whether injured or not, could improve their performance and gain enormous benefit from the Alexander Technique. This was the inspiration for the BodySense courses, which are designed specifically for riders who want to apply

Figure 1.1 You can see how the horse is attentive to his rider by the way his inside ear is tilted backward. The rider is nicely balanced and poised without excess tension. Both horse and rider give the impression that they are working in harmony with each other.

the Alexander Technique to their riding.

During a BodySense course, the first part of each day is spent on the ground, where riders learn to tune into their *kinesthetic* sense. They discover a "new way of going," by paying particular attention to the balance of the head and its relationship to the neck and back. At each step, the teacher uses her hands to guide the student's focus on and movement of the body and its responses.

Aspects of that student's posture and movement are explored in the chair, standing, walking, and lying down. Riders then receive individual attention on a wooden horse so that they can discuss problems in detail and changes can be made through guidance from the teacher's hands without the complications of a live horse moving under them. To encourage riders to explore these observations and increased awareness, riding sessions then take place on the longe at the walk. This is so that riders can learn to apply "*inhibition*" and "*direction*" (explained in Chapter Two, pages 22-23) while riding, and can become more conscious of habits that are hampering their riding ability. On the second day, trot work is included, after another unmounted session that explores balance and coordination. On the third day, riders learn to integrate their new skill and knowledge without the help of the longe. The aim is for riders to have an increased awareness of how to work on themselves so they can manage and change their own difficulties with greater efficiency.

Here are some comments I hear frequently from riders before they begin the course:

- "After half an hour of riding my back hurts."
- "My horse pulls me forward."
- "I can't sit at the trot and my legs grip upward."
- "I'm so nervous when I compete, how can I become more calm and poised?"
- "My horse doesn't move forward freely — am I gripping?"

The majority of these problems are the result of riders who have insufficient control of their own bodies. Typical examples of the types of riders coming to the BodySense courses are:

- Riders who recognise that they need more help to understand traditional teaching methods.
- Riders who have started riding again after a gap of several years and are not as supple as they used to be.
- Riders who suffer pain, either from injury or excessive tension.
- Dressage riders.
- Riding instructors who wish to improve their knowledge and understanding of the application of the rider's aids.
- Riders who wish to improve the welfare of the horse by correct, balanced riding.

Case History

Louise is a primary school teacher who has attended several Alexander Technique courses for riders. She took up riding in her fifties and acknowledged that she was nervous around horses. She thought if she could improve her balance and develop clearer communication with her horse, she might feel safer and become more confident. I watched Louise ride and observed how she sat in the saddle. She was crouching over, thus encouraging her horse to go faster, which in turn made her feel out of control.

As with all riders, I first put Louise in a saddle on a stationary, wooden horse. Free of the fear of unexpected movement, she was able to let me guide her to adopt a stable, upright position. The new position felt unfamiliar to her, especially when she was reunited with her horse on the longe line — the tendency to crouch forward was still there. Gradually, over some twenty minutes at the walk, Louise became more confident and her horse settled. The next day, as she

Figure 1.2 Louise's riding position before Alexander Technique lessons. Notice how she is tipping forward and rounding her back so that she is incapable of carrying her hands correctly. Her lower leg is too far back, which is increasing her tendency to throw her weight forward. If an imaginary line were drawn from the back of Louise's ear through her elbow, hip, and heel, it would not touch these joints. Note how Louise's head is poking forward.

Figure 1.3 Louise's position after Alexander lessons. Louise is much more balanced over her seat bones, her back is lengthened and her head and spine are more aligned. Although there is an increase in the bend at the elbow, the lower arm still needs to be carried higher. The lower leg is now helping to stablize the upper body by being underneath it.

began to grow more accustomed to her new upright position, she was able to start giving aids effectively and develop her riding skills further.

Louise says: "The course was a real revelation to me. I never realised how much excess tension I was holding in my body. I was using unnecessary effort not only in my riding, but in everyday life. Riding instructors had been trying to help me correct my posture, but I could never maintain the changes until I was given the experience of uprightness and balance by an Alexander Technique teacher. After further lessons my breathing became slower and deeper as a result of releasing tension and becoming less compressed. This gave me greater control and lightness in the saddle. BodySense has enabled me to feel confident and safe and now I have a much clearer understanding of how the horse's movement is influenced by my body" (figures 1.2 & 1.3).

Figure 1.4 Notice how Julie is tightening the neck and jaw muscles. The shoulders are tense and she is pulling her back muscles in and holding her breath. This makes the pelvis and thigh muscles tight so that she cannot sit deeply in the saddle. It looks as if Julie is holding her weight off the saddle.

Figure 1.5 Julie has released the tension in her neck and jaw, which has lessened the tension throughout the rest of her body. Note the softening in the shoulders and forearms and the improved suppleness in the seat and back muscles. Julie now looks as if she is sitting in the saddle rather than on it.

Case History

Julie is a qualified riding instructor who first came to me because of pain in her neck and shoulder that caused her to tighten her whole body. This tightness in turn caused a lack of suppleness that meant she was unable to use her back correctly, so Julie's horses were pulling against her hands. In order to counteract this, she became stuck in a spiral of excessive effort, increasing tension and pain that was hampering her riding ability.

Julie took a course of Alexander Technique lessons before her BodySense course. She began to realise that it was her poor coordination that had caused her back to become weak and compressed, which put strain on her shoulder and neck, causing pain. During her lessons, her back became more supple and her balance improved. In addition, the understanding she gained helped her to have a fresh appreciation of her pupils' difficulties (figures 1.4 & 1.5).

Julie says: "The Alexander Technique and BodySense have helped me gain increased awareness and control of my body so that now I can feel the horse's movement with greater accuracy. When I have difficulties with a horse, I can remain calm and maintain my position. Now I realise that nine times out of ten it is something I am doing with my body that is causing the horse to react adversely. My teaching is now much more effective as I am able to observe and understand how the whole body of the rider is affecting the horse's way of going. Rather than constantly trying to correct specific parts of the rider's body, I try to get to the root causes of the rider's problems, which is poor balance. With this approach pupils can progress more rapidly."

Despite their differences in riding ability, both Louise's and Julie's problems stemmed from the attitude that "if at first you don't succeed, try, try again." This well established advice in life does not always apply

Figure 1.6 The author encouraging greater freedom in a pupil's neck, with change in breathing and coordination.

in riding, because if you are using your body incorrectly in the first place, trying harder in the same manner merely repeats and compounds the existing *misuse*. BodySense helps the rider to become aware of habitual patterns of *misuse* of mind and body, therefore enabling her to eliminate excessive effort. This approach allows the body to find its natural poise and alertness, essential starting points for the serious rider.

What Happens During an Alexander Lesson?

When a person arrives for their first Alexander lesson, I usually try to find out what they would like to gain from a course of lessons. Often they have noticed changes in friends or partners who have learned the Alexander Technique. Such changes might be concerned with added calmness, or a change in posture and movement, or improved self-assurance. Not all Alexander students are riders, and I teach a variety of people who want to improve their performance, whether they are musicians, dancers or golfers. A number of people come to alleviate stress or pain, others have recurrent breathing problems. Increasingly riders are beginning to realise that a heightened awareness of their own bodies has a dramatic effect on their horses.

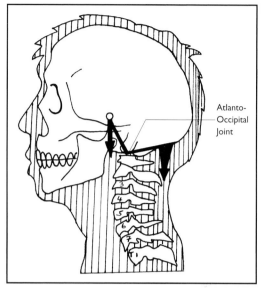

Figure 1.7 **The balance of the head and neck. Observe the center of gravity and the 7th cervical vertebra. This is where the majority of people think there is a joint but as you can see from the illustration it is not so.**

What follows is an overview of an Alexander lesson, to give you an idea of what is involved. It is not meant to be a "how to" manual, since the aid of a trained teacher's guiding hands is critical to successful mastering of the technique.

My goal is to help my students to become aware of any habits they have of reacting and tightening, which interfere with the freedom of movement through the head, neck, and back (figure 1.6).

I encourage students to remain "neutral" but alert, and not to anticipate movement, as this will bring about the usual habitual set of responses. The Alexander term for this control of anticipation is *inhibition*. In the beginning, most pupils have difficulty with the concept of *inhibition* since previous conditioning has taught them to react immediately. An important aspect of Alexander teaching is that you need to unlearn the harmful response before the new response can follow. As Alexander said, "How can the right things happen if we are still doing the wrong thing? Obviously we have to stop doing the wrong thing first."[2]

One of the first things a pupil does is to locate the *atlanto-occipital joint* (figure 1.7). Then I ask her to sit in an upright chair, so that I can place my hands on her neck. My hands help the pupil to become

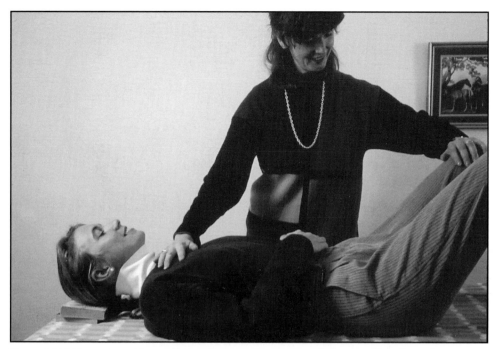

Figure 1.8 Table work enables pupils to release tension more easily because they do not have to cope with gravity. It also promotes a greater connection of the head, neck, and back.

more conscious of any tightening or inflexibility in the head, neck, and shoulders. Once the neck muscles are more free, most pupils are amazed to discover they can turn their heads much more easily, especially if they think of turning at the *atlanto-occipital joint*, rather than the region of the seventh cervical vertebra, lower down the neck.

Once awareness of the *atlanto-occipital joint* has increased, I ask my pupil to take her attention to the sitting bones so that she can begin to direct her thinking from this base of support to the head, neck, and back again. Most people are not really conscious of their back muscles and this process helps to increase their awareness.

With my hands still in contact with my pupil's neck, I ask her to stand up in her usual fashion. Once upright, we discuss how the body is organised to carry out this activity. Most students are surprised to find that they have no accurate idea of what is actually happening! This is just one example of an activity that everyone carries out numerous times a day, yet they *misuse* themselves in the process. Misusing the body produces excess tension, which restricts breathing and compresses the joints and vital organs. Most pupils' reaction to misusing the body is to "put it right" by overreacting, which adds more tension to the underlying *misuse* and stress. During the lesson, I have the student lie down on a table as a good antidote to "overdoing." While the

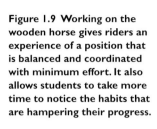

Figure 1.9 Working on the wooden horse gives riders an experience of a position that is balanced and coordinated with minimum effort. It also allows students to take more time to notice the habits that are hampering their progress.

pupil is lying down, I use my hands to encourage release of tension in the neck and back muscles. I watch to see if my pupil's breathing becomes slower and deeper or more rhythmical. I then work on each leg separately. Pupils often feel it is difficult to give me the weight of each leg, and the more tightness is present, the harder it is to let go (figure 1.8).

I do not expect miracles the first time — if the hip joint and surrounding muscles release to some degree I am happy. Next, I work on the arms much as I did with the legs. I want to enhance the connection through the neck and back muscles, so that the shoulder muscles, which are habitually overused, have a chance to let go. This affects the pectoral muscles and therefore breathing capacity. Throughout the lesson I pay attention to the manner in which I use my own body because this also will have an effect on my pupil.

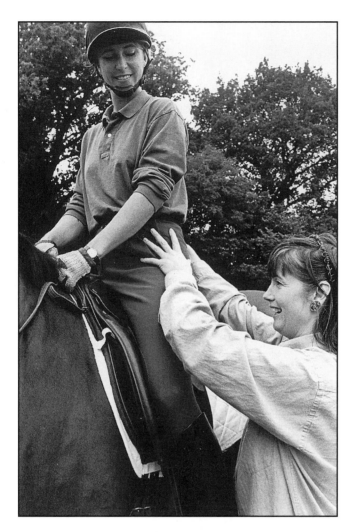

Figure 1.10 Encouraging *good use* of the muscles around the pelvis and hips helps riders to become aware of their breathing and weight distribution in the saddle.

After the table work, I observe a riding student as she sits in a saddle on a wooden horse, so that she can discuss her position and any difficulties she may incur while riding. These discussions can then be referred to during the BodySense courses (figure 1.9).

I then use my hands to bring about a change in tension distributed throughout the body. Most pupils remark that they have never managed to sit so deeply or felt their legs so long (figure 1.10).

Alexander teachers train full time for three years. A part of the training teaches them to convey new correct sensory experiences to the pupil's body so that the over-analytical tendencies of the mind can be overcome. The hands have a huge advantage over verbal instruction since they teach the pupil how to tune into the *kinesthetic* sense. Some pupils have more difficulty getting in touch with their bodies than others. However, after a varying number of lessons, most students re-

Figure 1.11 Driving a car is often a source of tension. Notice how the shoulders are tight and how the driver is gripping the steering wheel. She is likely to be holding her breath, which magnifies tension as well.

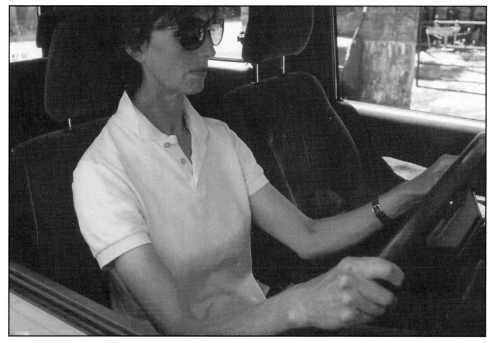

Figure 1.12 The driver looks so much more relaxed, her shoulders are freer and not hunched forward. Her arms are holding the steering wheel securely, yet with the appropriate amount of effort. In this position, the driver will be far less over-reactive.

port greater awareness, lightness, and ease of movement. Pupils often change shape and look more at ease within themselves.

Lessons usually last thirty- to forty-minutes. As a pupil improves, various activities might be introduced during lessons. Pupils often bring in their musical instruments, tennis rackets, and golf clubs. Teachers have become passengers in cars and have gone swimming and riding (figures 1.11 & 1.12).

In Alexander's time, pupils came for lessons six days a week for approximately one month. Alexander said this was the most satisfactory way of teaching, as old habits could be kept in check while fragile new improved coordinations became more established. Nowadays it is difficult for pupils to find the time to take an intensive course of lessons and, as a result, many teachers recommend twice weekly lessons for the first five or six weeks, followed by once weekly lessons thereafter.

The Technique is like learning a language; you can refine it as much as you like. However, a basic course of 25 to 30 lessons is recommended so that you can apply Alexander principles to your everyday life. The benefit that is derived from lessons is that they enable you to manage yourself and your life more efficiently and with less effort, so it really is a superb investment. Lessons help pupils to develop greater awareness of their *kinesthetic* sense, which is highly desirable for riders.

In the following chapter I will give an explanation of the Alexander Technique and how it affects the way we use our bodies. This will give you a deeper understanding as to how "BodySense" was evolved and how crucial the Technique and its philosophies are to riders.

2

The Alexander Technique

F.M. Alexander – Founder of the Alexander Technique

Frederick Matthias Alexander, the originator of the Alexander Technique, was born in 1869 and grew up as a sickly child on a remote farm in Tasmania, Australia. His mother bred horses and was a keen rider, his father was a farrier. From an early age Alexander devoted himself to horses, and later becoming involved in training them.

Alexander had also developed a passion for Shakespeare, and decided to pursue a career in mainland Australia as a full-time actor and recitalist. This became impossible when he began to experience a recurring hoarseness and loss of voice. He consulted voice experts, but they could find nothing wrong and advised him simply to rest. His voice did return, only for the problem to recur at the next attempted performance. Frustrated and disturbed that he could only gain temporary relief, he returned to the voice expert who agreed with Alexander's analysis that he must be using his voice in the wrong way when performing. There was no known solution to this problem at that time.

Alexander decided to take this unpromising situation into his own hands and embarked on a long, painstaking, and thorough investigation of his voice. His investigations resulted in a series of important discoveries that enabled him to find the solution to his hoarseness. He wrote a full account of his discoveries in his book, *The Use of the Self*, which was first published in 1932. His voice and breathing recovered to such an extent that his fellow performers asked for his advice. He became so successful in helping them that he embarked on a new career, teaching what was later to become known as the Alexander Technique.

By 1904, Alexander had built up a good teaching practice in

Figure 2.1
F.M. Alexander had a great passion for horses.

Sydney and was encouraged to take his new technique to London by Dr. Stewart McKay, a well-known surgeon. He started attracting the rich and famous, especially those from the theatre world.

At the outbreak of war in 1914, he set sail for America. Again he attracted influential figures and built up another successful practice. From 1918 to 1924, Alexander regularly spent one half of the year in London and the other half in America. His busy practice in Boston was maintained by his brother Arthur Reddon, whom Alexander had trained in Australia.

Alexander retained his interest in horses and continued riding regularly all his life, both on his estate in Bexley, Kent and in Hyde Park, London. He taught his Technique until a week before he died in 1955 at the age of 86 (figure 2.1).

The Primary Control

Alexander had no previous experience with studying the human body when he began his years of self-observation. He was a practical man who came to the subject with a fresh outlook, uncluttered by other people's theories and ideas. He had little time for armchair theorists, preferring to use practical experiments as the basis for his study. Like the trainer who needs to watch his horse in movement in order to study the quality of its gaits, Alexander had to observe himself while reciting to discover what was happening to his voice.

He noticed three distinct recurring patterns, which he described "as a tendency to pull the head back, depress the larynx, and suck in breath."[3] He suspected that this might be a "*misuse*" of his body since it seemed to compress his spine and pull in his torso, so he set about preventing it from happening. To his surprise, this wasn't as easy to do as he thought. After months of further experiment he found that if he could stop the pulling back of the head, to some extent this indirectly checked the sucking in of breath and the depressing of the larynx, and his voice and the stiffening in his body improved. He was convinced that he had found the cause of his problem and he was encouraged to continue his observations. This subsequently resulted in his significant discovery.

Alexander believed he had broken new ground by detecting that the relationship of his head and neck to his back not only influenced the functioning of his vocal mechanisms, but seemed to play a central role in the balance and coordination of his entire body. The balance of the head and its relationship to the neck and back he called "*primary control*" and felt that it was the answer to developing efficient use of the body in all activities.

The Significance of the Primary Control for Riders

Alexander's *primary control* — the balance of the head and its relationship to the neck and back — gives riders a guiding principle that they can use to restore their body's natural ability to remain easily balanced and upright (figure 2.2). Riders spend a great deal of time learning about their horse's equilibrium, but have very little knowledge of how their own bodies are designed to be balanced and used effectively. Through releasing the muscles in the neck, riders can learn how to engage their back muscles properly to provide an upward direction, which lengthens their stature and improves alignment. The release of the neck and back muscles, helps to encourage greater freedom in the rib cage, and breathing capacity is enhanced. The Alexander

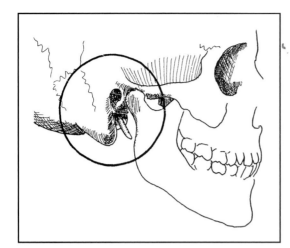

Figure 2.2 The relationship of the atlanto-occipital region to the head and neck. The area circled is the most important, the primary area to consider in dealing with the balance of the body as a whole. Here, lie the semicircular canals detecting changes in the head's position, parts of the brain stem having to do with muscle tone, reflexes and balance, the fulcrum of the head on the neck (the atlanto-occipital joint), the hinge of the jaw, and the mastoid and styloid processes from which radiate multitudious muscle and ligament connections. Thus there is an intimate relationship between this area and all the surrounding structures: the tongue, jaw, hyoid bone, larynx, trachea, esophagus, clavicle, ribs, sternum, and scapula. The processes of eating, breathing, swallowing, talking, singing, seeing, and hearing all originate from this area. (Courtesy of David Gorman.)

Technique teaches pupils to undo tensions that are interfering with balance and coordination instead of forcing the body into what is perceived as an ideal shape. BodySense teaches you to apply these principles while on a horse (figure 2.3).

Like the changes brought about during the training of horses, good movement by the rider cannot be forced. Improvement takes place over a period of time on a mental and physical level. Changes made in Alexander lessons and during dressage training both involve reorganisation of the head-neck-back relationship, which alters as balance improves. When this relationship is functioning well, the quality of movement is affected by the even distribution of muscle tone throughout the body so that less effort is required for the movement. Alexander called this "*good use.*"

Riders who display *good use* are far more likely to create a harmonious relationship with the horse. They are balanced and in control of their movements, which are lighter and freer than a rider who may be using herself wrongly. Unfortunately, most riders are less familiar with observing *good use* in themselves than in their horses.

Developing the Connection of the Head, Neck, and Back
The relationship between the head, neck, and back is crucial for governing the body's balance and coordination, but many riders lack awareness of how the head balances on top of the spine. Look at the illustration of the *atlanto-occipital joint* (page 7) to help locate this joint on yourself, first find your jaw joint (figure 2.4). Now, keeping your fingers as close as possible to the ear, trace down and around to the back of the ear, stopping halfway up. Nod your head while you imagine a dowel running between your ears. This is where your head sits on top of the spine. Ask yourself if you normally move from this joint.

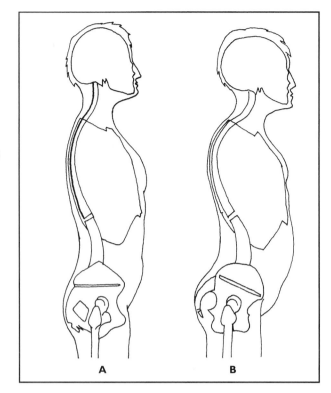

Figure 2.3 Notice how the shortening of the neck in figure B affects the overall stature by compressing the spine and tilting the angle of the pelvis. The back looks hollow compared to figure A.

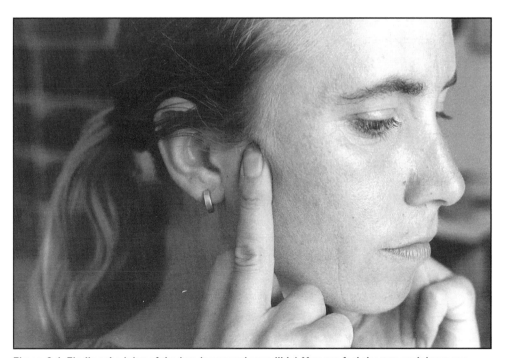

Figure 2.4 Finding the joint of the jaw (temporal mandible). You can feel the two nodules move when you gently open your mouth.

Many riders drop their heads from the base of the neck, from the seventh cervical vertebra (see figure 1.7, page 7). This means that the deep postural muscles of the back are not adequately engaged to keep the head easily poised on top of the spine. There is insufficient tone through the back, and as a result the head disturbs the balance throughout the body.

Effects of Fear

The superficial muscles of the neck are the first to react in times of fear and emergency. For example, if someone needs to defend herself, or needs to escape, these muscles tighten so that the head retracts and the shoulders rise in a defensive and protective posture, indicating fear. This starts as a temporary state, but with repeated experiences it is likely to become locked into the musculature of the body. It is a sad fact that the pressures of living in a modern Western society cause many people to respond as if they were in a situation of emergency most of the time. This produces a constant state of underlying tension, muscular over-activity, and a general shortening of stature. As a result, the appropriate distribution of muscle tone through the body is impeded. The limbs tend to do too much, while the back, which has the most powerful muscles in the body, does too little. Without sufficient support from the back, the human body will be locked into an ever-increasing battle to stay upright. A similar cycle of tension takes place in the horse.

The horse is a creature of flight and is easily alarmed. When anxious, its automatic response is to raise its head and hollow its back. The weight of a rider may cause the same reaction unless a young horse is well prepared. The trainer's task is to educate the horse to avoid this automatic response, so that the head–neck–back relationship can effectively balance the horse in his work. This makes it easier for the rider to sit on top and control the horse. The horse must be trained correctly so that he has enough tone in the neck to balance the head and lighten the forehand without interfering with the suppleness at the poll.

A horse with conformation that predisposes him to weakness and injury needs correct riding and training if his working life is to be preserved. A correctly balanced rider will help the horse to balance himself. A rider who realises how her own and her horse's innate balance and coordination are organised around the relationship of the head, neck, and back *(primary control)* has taken the first step to achieving that lightness and poise sought by all riders. But many people have difficulty in allowing the *primary control* to function effectively.

The Use of Self

Because of the novelty and complexity of his revolutionary perspective, F.M. Alexander needed to find suitable words to describe the concepts he was introducing. He chose "*use,*" which covers a person's total pattern of behaviour and reaction to a stimulus at any given time. Movement, posture, and gesture are external manifestations of *use.* Alexander realised that any physical movement or activity must include the working of both mind and body. He used the word "psycho-physical" to embrace this principle, which underpinned his technique. Although mind-body unity is a fashionable concept nowadays, in Alexander's time it was considered eccentric.

Good Use

"*Good use*" is a well-balanced head–neck–back relationship *(primary control)* allowing for coordination, freedom, and ease of movement distributed appropriately throughout the body. This can only be achieved by the adoption of the psycho-physical approach. Riders need to become increasingly more aware of their reactions to outside influences. Through the Alexander Technique and BodySense we can improve our "*good use*" and therefore our horsemanship.

Misuse

"*Misuse*" will usually originate from the malfunctioning of the *primary control* as it did in Alexander's experience of pulling back his head, sucking in his breath, and depressing his larynx, all of which had a detrimental effect on his voice and performance. In some areas of the body there may be an excessive degree of muscular tension and effort compensating for poor *use* elsewhere. We can learn to identify *good use* and *misuse*, and it is essential for riders to do so in order to arrest the development of damaging *habits*. The first step is to recognize the habitual ways we move, react, and carry ourselves.

Recognising Habit in Riders

Habits by their very nature are subconscious, automatic responses. F.M. Alexander considered all *habits* to have a "psycho-physical" basis. They are neither wholly physical nor wholly mental for what is exhibited in the body is inextricably linked to the mind, and vice versa.

A young child learns to move by developing the relevant neuro-muscular pathways for crawling, and then progresses to standing and walking (figures 2.5-2.7). Notice how the young child stands so poised. Sadly, by the time the child becomes an adult the pressures of modern

Figure 2.5 Children naturally use their hips, knees, and ankle joints until they spend long hours sitting and studying at school. Gradually over a period of time their bodies stiffen up and they forget how easily they once moved.

Figure 2.6 Notice how easily the child stands upright and how large her head is in comparison to the rest of her body.

day living have taken their toll. The demands made by various occupations for which the body is not designed cause disharmony between the physical and mental, and bad *habits* can develop. Riding will show up such poor coordination, but unfortunately it usually feels so familiar that it becomes increasingly difficult to change. An example of this is the effect on our bodies of being left- or right-handed. Most people find that the entire left or right side of the body is stronger and more coordinated than the other side.

You can carry out a simple check to find if you are constantly using one side of your body more than the other. Ask yourself which hand you use to pick up the telephone. And which ear do you use to listen to the voice on the other end? Do you use the same hand to brush your teeth, put a key in the lock, open the door, carry a bucket, and so forth? These simple observations can be valuable, because they show you how a *habit* pattern forms even when you are unaware of it. By repeating the activity in the same way, you are programming the pathways from your brain to your body, building up a favoured response that will eventually become automatic.

Figure 2.7 Observe the natural poise, confidence, and balance inherent in this young rider. She looks really at home despite the fact that her pony is rather large for her.

Try folding your arms in front of you. Then unfold them and fold them the other way around. The first way is likely to be your favoured way, and the second will probably seem unfamiliar and more difficult. You can try the same experiment by crossing your legs. One way will feel more comfortable than the other depending on which way you usually cross them.

You can see how these *habits* can affect the body by looking in a mirror. Is one shoulder or hip higher than the other? Is your head tilted to one side? Do you drop the shoulders forward or pull them back? Does the upper body lean too far forward or backward? The shape and alignment of the body can reveal external symptoms of *misuse*.

Inhibition

Did you know that simply thinking about an activity triggers a muscular response? If you take time to observe yourself before doing a familiar activity, you may notice that you tense your neck muscles or hold your breath, yet you are not normally aware of doing so. Muscles often become set or programmed into habitual ways of responding. Alexander realised that if he wanted to change his immediate reaction to a stimulus (tightening of muscles), he would have to get himself to stop the reaction before it occurred. He called this stopping or pausing "*inhibition*." (This use of the term has nothing to do with Sigmund Freud's psychoanalytical interpretation of the word.) Learning to inhibit stops us from becoming slaves to *habit* and gives us a real choice of actions. *Inhibition* is the key to the removal of unwanted habitual reactions to a stimulus. This is important because otherwise you are only overlaying one wrong *habit* pattern on top of another. As Alexander says in *Man's Supreme Inheritance*, "It is therefore obvious that the correct order of procedure for teacher and pupil is first for the pupil to learn to prevent himself from doing the wrong things which causes imperfections or defects, and then, as a secondary consideration in procedure, to learn the correct way to use the mental and physical mechanism concerned."[4]

A good rider's main attribute in addition to skill is a calmness that allows her time to monitor both her own and her horse's responses. Like a horse who needs to be settled before it can learn anything, so a rider needs to be in a similar state if she is to respond and interpret her horse's actions appropriately. A rider who overreacts disturbs the horse's balance and locomotion.

Let's again look at an example from daily life. The next time you hear the telephone ring, notice if you rush to it automatically, or if you can actually take a few seconds to decide whether you want to answer or not. Pausing for a moment or two can actually help you to become more conscious of the quality of your response, both in thinking and in activity.

Most riders find it difficult to put this thought process into practice when they are actually on the horse. "The good rider is not he who, seeing resistances and serious difficulties appear in a new exercise, tries to conquer them at any price, sometimes using violence and brutality, but rather he who, on seeing the resistance rise up, knows how to return to the beginning, to the preparatory exercises, until he has obtained the flexibility and relaxation necessary to start the exercise he is trying to teach."[5]

Once F.M. Alexander found that before he spoke he could "inhibit" his immediate reaction of tightening his neck and pulling his head back, he then realised that he had to redirect the use of himself in order to totally counteract this *habit* of *misuse*. He therefore devised a "set of orders to project to himself" while still inhibiting his first reaction. He called these "*directions*."

Directions

We are actually directing our actions all the time, but in most cases the *directions* from the mind to the body have become so automatic that they are subconscious. Often we are not aware of how we may be carrying out certain activities. For example, a lot of people are not aware of the chain of reactions that occur when they get up from a chair, yet it is a movement they carry out many times a day. Alexander realised that by giving himself *directions*, he was helping to prevent *misuse* of the *primary control*.

The *directions* Alexander devised are as follows:
"Let the neck be free so that the back can lengthen and widen and the head can go forward and up and the knees forward and away."[6] Remember that these are preventative *directions* and are **thoughts**, not **actions**. Many Alexander pupils try to "do" these *directions* since they have difficulty believing that thinking alone can work.

It is very important to remember that *direction* is no good without *inhibition*. *Inhibition* and *direction* could be compared with a half-halt, where the horse makes a momentary pause in response to the rider's aids. The half-halt is then followed by an aid that "directs" the horse in its new improved balance. A half-halt is also used for focusing the horse's attention and as a preparation for a change in pace. What Alexander discovered was that we are very much like our horses: we need to pause or inhibit the unwanted response to a stimulus, then give ourselves *directions* to carry out a new movement with the correct *use* of the body through improved functions of the *primary control*.

Developing Inhibition and
Direction in the Semi-Supine Position

The semi-supine position is used by many Alexander teachers and students because it allows them to become aware of the excess tension that has built up in their bodies. The following procedure will help you to experience the benefit of this position. Find a quiet, warm place on a carpeted floor.

Place two or three paperback books on the carpet behind you,

Figure 2.8 The semi-supine position. Carefully lower yourself onto the floor into a sitting position. Make sure the weight is even on both seat bones, both hands, and both feet.

and then carefully lower yourself onto the floor into a sitting position; make sure your weight is even on both seat bones, both hands, and both feet (figure 2.8).

Gently lean back onto your elbows, keeping your feet on the floor, knees toward the ceiling. Lift your pelvis, and move it in the direction of your feet (figure 2.9).

Let your elbows slide away from your body as your back unrolls onto the floor. Keep your feet flat on the floor and knees bent. Adjust the books behind you so that they support the back of your head. The books need to be high enough to prevent your head from tipping back, but not so high that your chin and throat are constricted. Your whole body is now completely supported by the floor. Notice how much contact your back has with the floor (figures 2.10 & 2.11).

Think of releasing your neck muscles to allow the head to be completely supported by the books. Then think of allowing your back to lengthen and widen, and of your arms and legs connecting to your back. Notice your breathing and allow it to become deeper and slower so that your body releases and your mind can become still. Take some time to "center yourself" — notice if your mind is with your body or racing ahead to your next activity. You can lie down like this for ten to fifteen minutes every day as a way of directing your mind to become

Figure 2.9 Lean back onto your elbows, lift your pelvis a fraction, and move it in the direction of your feet. Now let your elbows slide away from your body as your back unrolls onto the floor.

Figure 2.10 Allow your whole body to be completely supported by the floor. Notice how much contact your back has with the floor and allow your breathing to become deeper and slower.

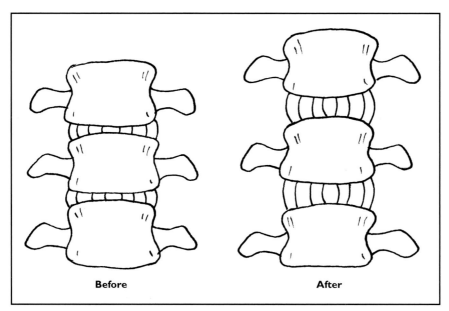

Before   **After**

Figure 2.11 The intervertebral discs before and after lying down. It's surprising how much more space can be seen between the discs in a supine position.

aware of the excess tension in your body. As the mind becomes aware of these tensions you will be able to use *inhibition* and *direction* to bring about a change. This will allow the body and mind to work together in harmony, helping to make your riding lessons less frustrating and more rewarding.

Endgaining

These days most people have become so focused on obtaining goals that they do not realise how much they might be harming themselves in the process. This exclusive focusing on goals Alexander called "*endgaining.*" He believed that this stood in the way of maintaining a high standard of health and being able to use ourselves economically. He said, "when a person has reached a given stage of unsatisfactory *use* and functioning, his *habit* of *endgaining* will prove to be the impeding factor in all his attempts to profit by any teaching method whatsoever."[7]

Mean Whereby

Most current methods of physical and mental education teach pupils to concentrate solely on achieving end results. Exams, for example, often create pressures and body tension. Most importantly they ignore the power of *habit*. Alexander was not against having clear goals, as observed in his book *The Use of the Self*, but, he believed that how you journey is vital to the ultimate arrival. In other words, if you pay attention to the process the outcome will improve as a result.

Paying attention to the steps involved in reaching whatever goal you have set for yourself is known in Alexander jargon as "*means whereby.*" A rider who is able to focus on the *means whereby* is much more likely to build a successful rapport with her horse because it means she has taken the time to create a dialogue.

Show jumping can be used as a prime example of *means whereby* in action. Most jumping faults occur as a result of the way the approach is ridden, when the rider's mind is preoccupied with the actual jumping of the fence (*endgaining*) and not with her balance in harmony with the horse. Riding a course of jumps accurately is a perfect example of Alexander's concept of *means whereby* because as it is the approach that will govern the result.

3

The Alexander Technique and Riding

As you saw in the case studies described in Chapter One, BodySense teaching helps to improve a rider's state of mind, awareness, balance, and ease of movement. She learns that the way she sits on her horse can either enhance or restrict the horse's ability to perform. The rider's attitude also has a huge impact because it is mirrored in her body and therefore picked up by her horse. Many riders are unaware to what extent their body influences the horse. The majority focus solely on the horse without giving themselves a thought! Horses mirror their riders' tension patterns to an extraordinary degree.

BodySense teaching can help to create greater unity between horse and rider. It gives riders more choice in how to react in varying circumstances, thereby increasing physical and mental awareness and sensitivity. *Habits* that have been hampering progress can be overcome. Applying the Alexander Technique with the help of BodySense encourages the rider to ride in greater harmony with the horse, who in turn responds more favourably, and whose carriage and coordination improve. There is no other art or sport where an animal is so involved in the process of change — who better than the horse to confirm the rider's progress? BodySense can build a rider's awareness of how the body is designed to function and how mobility is diminished by excessive tightening and contracting.

Locating Your Joints

"Body mapping" is a term used by Bill and Barbara Conable, American teachers of the Alexander Technique who specialise in teaching

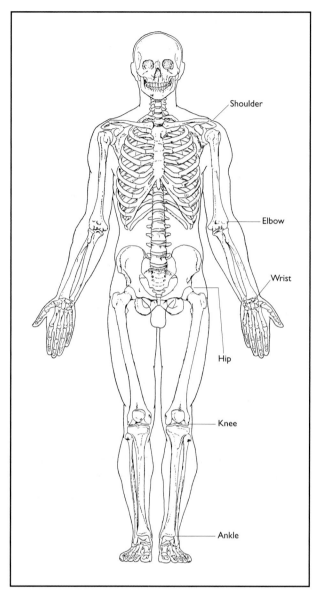

Shoulder

Elbow

Wrist

Hip

Knee

Ankle

Figure 3.1 It's a good idea to know exactly where your joints are located. Look at the main joints: shoulder, elbow, wrist, hip, knee, ankle.

musicians and actors.[8] They discovered that people will move according to how they perceive their structure. Everyone possesses an internal map of themselves that does not necessarily correlate with reality. You can experiment to see how your body map corresponds to your personal concept by drawing yourself in skeleton form and marking all the joints.

Joints are the sites at which two or more bones meet. There are many different kinds of joints with varying degrees of movement.

• Fibrous joints are attached by fibrous connective tissue. The virtually immovable flat bones of the skull are joined in this way.

• Cartilaginous joints are connected by cartilage connective tissue reinforced with fibrous tissue, such as the discs between vertebrae, which are partly movable.

• Synovial joints have a smooth cartilage gliding surface on the bone ends, and are surrounded by a fibrous capsule interlaced with ligaments. There are two main types of synovial joint: the ball and socket and the hinge. In the ball and socket, the round end of the bone fits into the socket-like head of another bone, which allows maximum movement, as in the shoulder and the hip joint. In the hinge joints, such as the elbow or ankle, a hinge-like action allows one bone to swing around the other (figure 3.1).

Knowing where joints are in theory does not mean that they will be used correctly in practice. Try the following activities to see how well you know where your joint can be found.

Joints Involved in Taking Rein Contact

Sitting on a chair, put your arms in front of you as if you are taking up the reins, with a 90-degree angle at the elbow. Notice if the weight has changed on your seat bones or if there is movement in any other part of the body. For example, does your upper body sway back or do your shoulders rise? Now take your hands down and think of your fingertips leading the movement before repeating the procedure. Notice how the elbow creates the bend and less effort is needed throughout the body. Many riders unconsciously contract their arms as they take up the reins, causing other areas, such as the neck and shoulders, to become unnecessarily tight, which interferes with a consistent contact.

The Upper Arm and Shoulder

Now, with the arms hanging straight down to the fingertips, swing your arm back and forth like a pendulum. Which joint is being used now? Your shoulder is the only joint involved. Do you imagine the joint to be on the point of the shoulder or by the shoulder blades? (figure 3.2)

To find your shoulder joint, use a mirror and place your right hand underneath your left armpit with the left hand resting by your side. Without lifting the right shoulder or collapsing your side, let the weight drop down the arm to the fingertips, then move the arm slowly backward and forward (figure 3.3).

Can you feel what happens to the joint under-

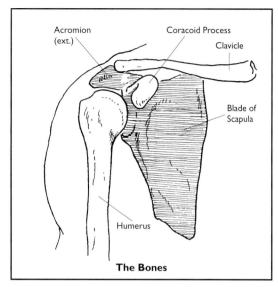

Figure 3.2 The shoulder joint is situated more deeply underneath the acromion than most people think.

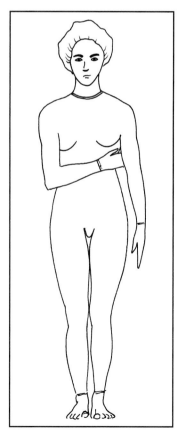

Figure 3.3 Discovering how the shoulder joint can move without involving excess tension in the biceps.

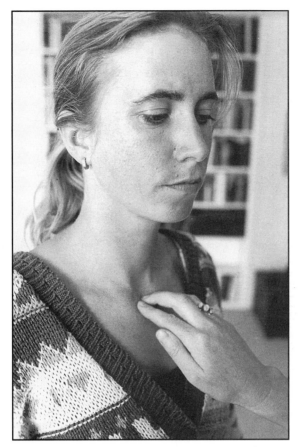

Figure 3.4 Finding your clavicle joint is important for shoulder and arm awareness.

neath the armpit? This ball and socket joint has plenty of potential for movement in all directions, but it is often blocked by tension as riders aren't really conscious of the actual location of the shoulder joint.

Now put your arms by your sides, circle both shoulders clockwise then counterclockwise. Now find your clavicle joint (figure 3.4).

Place your finger on this joint and repeat circling each shoulder. Do you notice the range of motion? Now stop circling, but take one hand above your head and notice that there is movement in the clavicle. Although not classed as a "proper joint," if the clavicle were fixed, the amount of freedom in the shoulders would be restricted. How many joints are involved in holding the reins? Most riders will answer three: wrist, elbow, and shoulder. It is important to recognise that the clavicle brings the total to four. Taking account of this will affect the way you use your arms and therefore your rein contact.

Lower Arm Awareness

Allowing your arms to hang by your side, turn your palms to face forward (little finger on the inside). Take the lower arm up so that it forms a right angle at the elbow. Make sure that the elbow is not clamped to your side, but is hanging loosely. Do this slowly several times. Are you aware of holding your breath and involving the shoulder joint or can the lower arm bend solely from the elbow joint? Elbow joints are important because they affect the quality of the rein contact (figure 3.5). If the muscles connected around the elbow are tight, they will block the free flow of energy created by the horse's hindquarters that needs to travel through the horse's body and to the rider's hands from the bit (figure 3.6).

Figure 3.5 Elbow joints are important for consistent elastic rein contact. Here the author helps to encourage greater freedom in the joint and the muscles surrounding it.

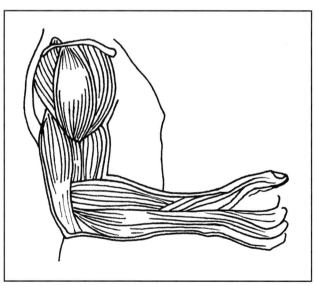

Figure 3.6 Notice how the muscles of the upper arm and elbow interlink and affect the hand.

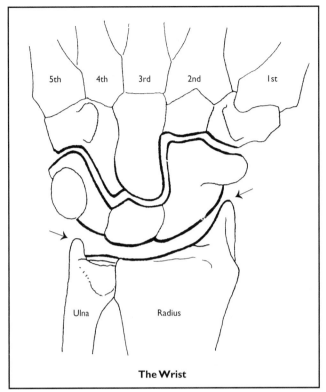

5th   4th   3rd   2nd   1st

Ulna   Radius

The Wrist

Figure 3.7 The radius and ulna bones of the wrist also affect the quality of rein contact.

Wrist Joint Awareness

Supple wrist joints are also crucial for an elastic rein contact. If the wrist joint is stiff, it will break the flow of communication to the horse's mouth. The hand will then become heavy and fixed. Locate the position of your radius and ulna (figure 3.7). Massage the wrist joint. Trace the finger joints from the wrist. Notice any tension in the fingers (figure 3.8).

Now sit down and support the lower arm from the elbow to the fingers, on a table with the hand on its side, thumb uppermost. Make sure the line from the elbow to fingertips is straight (figure 3.9).

Now open and close the hand without lifting it off the table. Does this movement happen from your wrist or the joints in your hand? Take care not to disturb the line to the elbow. Place the thumb from your right hand into the middle of your left palm and find the joints toward the center of the hand. Now move your fingers. The joint at the base of the fingers is already more toward the palm than you might think. Fingers are not only jointed from the knuckles. The tendency to tighten the wrist increases if you think of the fingers bending on the outside of the hand. Thinking of bending the fingers on the inside will increase elasticity in rein contact. The palm of the hand needs to be supple, otherwise the hand will be bent awkwardly and the wrist will be stiff.

Hip Joint

You can locate the hip joint by standing against a wall and lifting the knee. With your fingertips, find the point at which the leg joins the pelvis. Note that these joints are not the bumps on the top of the thigh that most people refer to as their hips. The hip joints are located well

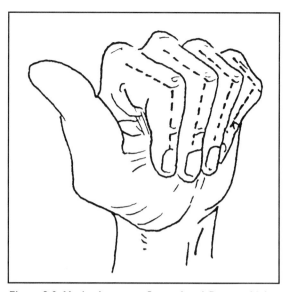

Figure 3.8 Notice how your fingers bend. Do you think of them bending from the knuckles on the outside of the hand, or do you create a bend more from the inside around your palm?

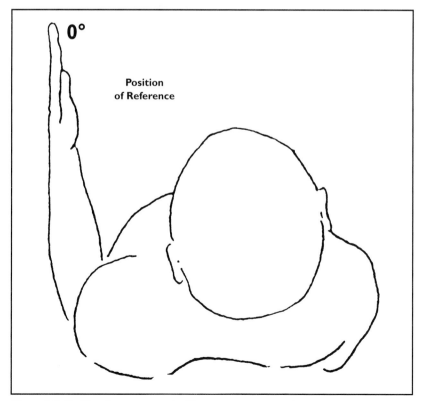

Figure 3.9 Position for assessment of lower arm movement.

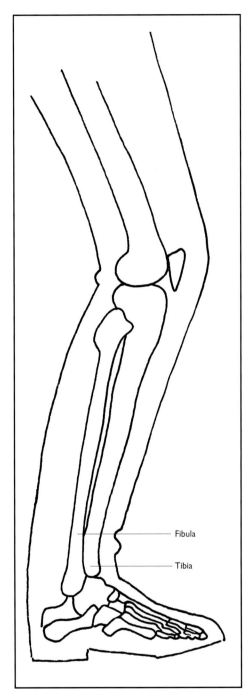

Fibula

Tibia

Figure 3.10 Think of the ankle joint bending upward from underneath the foot. This allows greater rotation on the point where the tibia and fibula meet. Ankle joints need to be relaxed to absorb the horse's movement.

inside the body, as the illustration shows (see page 30, figure 3.1). Move away from the wall and try swinging the leg gently backward and forward and from side to side to experience the range of possible movement of this joint. Make sure you are keeping your upper body erect so that you are not collapsing down onto one hip. The correct understanding of the hip joint location is essential both for the balance of the upper body and freedom of the legs in the saddle.

Lower Leg and Foot
To become aware of your knee joint, sit astride a high chair and swing the lower leg back and forth like a pendulum. Think of the toes taking the knee forward and the heel taking the knee back. This movement should come from the knee and hip while the ankle remains soft. Make sure that the calf muscle is relaxed.

Ankle Joint Awareness
Look at the illustration of the ankle joint (figure 3.10). The point where the tibia and fibula meet is often referred to as the ankle joint. However, the bones in the foot also govern the flexibility in this joint. Tap your fingers underneath the foot and over the top of the arch to help you release any tension in this area.

You can "tune in" to your ankles and feet if you take your shoes off and walk around the room. Then imagine that you are walking on sand. Stand on your left leg and raise your right knee so that the right toes curl and make contact with the floor (figure 3.11). Now walk forward as if you are drawing a line through sand with the curled top of your big toe (figure 3.12). Take several more steps like

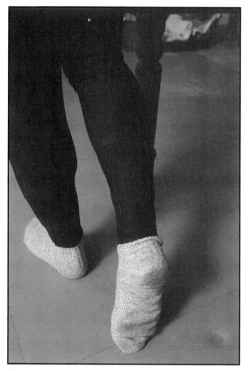 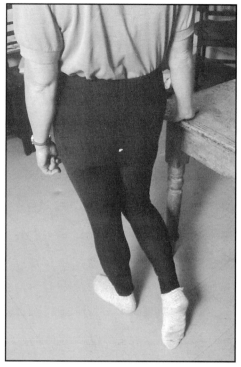

Figure 3.11 Imagine that you are dragging your toes through sand so that the knee leads the movement of the flexed toe.

Figure 3.12 Take care that you do not tip or twist the pelvis or drop the weight into the supporting leg by bending at the knee.

this and then walk normally. Take care not to push the pelvis forward. Notice how the muscles over the top of the ankles have to soften to allow your toes to remain in contact with the floor. (It is best to do this on a soft surface, or better still on the beach!) Think of the knee leading the foot. Be careful not to draw the knees up and make sure your toes remain in contact with the floor. This can also help with softening the calf muscles. What do you notice? Are your feet in better contact with the floor? Are your calf muscles softer and your ankles more flexible? When you next sit in the saddle, think of pivoting the foot upward from the muscles underneath the instep as well as the ankle. This helps to release the muscles over the top of the ankle.

You will need a partner to try another procedure that encourages flexibility in the hips, knees, and ankle joints. Stand facing each other comfortably, feet apart, holding hands with arms outstretched. Now move backward until your arms are almost straight but there is still a slight bend at the elbow. Gently lean back from the ankle joints so that each person is gaining support from the other. The arms need to be almost straight and the body needs to be pivoted backward in one piece from the ankle joints (figure 3.13).

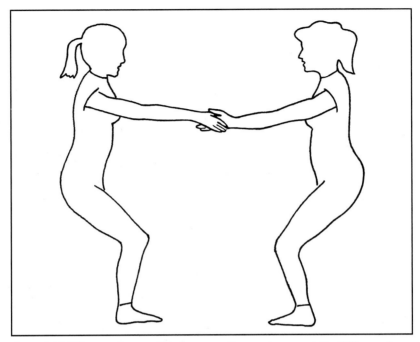

Figure 3.13 This experiment will help you to discover how much flexibility you have in your hips, knees, and ankles. Make sure you counterbalance each others' weight and think of the support coming to the arms via the back.

Keep a slight bend at the elbow and take care that the hips are not thrust forward. Think of the support coming from you back through your arms. Still keeping the same amount of supporting tension through each other's arms and body, release the knees forward so that both of you increase the bend in your hips, knees, and ankles as you get closer to the floor. If you can, take care that you don't pull each other forward as you lower your center of gravity. Reorganise, keeping your weight backwards, before you come up again. This procedure helps you to gain awareness of the degree of flexibility or, in some cases, inflexibility in your joints.

Finding Your Seat Bones

"It is only when we genuinely attempt to preserve our balance by suppleness and poise rather than strength of grip that we realise how difficult it is to distribute our weight equally on both seat bones"
from *The Way to Perfect Horsemanship* by Udo Bürger.[9]

Try this experiment to see how well balanced you are. Begin by sitting in a chair. Put one hand under each seat bone and notice if the weight

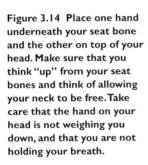

Figure 3.14 Place one hand underneath your seat bone and the other on top of your head. Make sure that you think "up" from your seat bones and think of allowing your neck to be free. Take care that the hand on your head is not weighing you down, and that you are not holding your breath.

of your seat bones is evenly distributed on each hand. Make sure your pelvis is not tilted and check that both feet are flat on the floor. Remind yourself of the *atlanto-occipital joint* (see figure 2.2, page 16). Think of your head being free to move on the top vertebrae. Now move your head to the right and then to the left. Can you detect how this affects the evenness on your seat bones? What happens to your back? Does it fold in the middle? What happens to your head and neck? Now take one hand from underneath your seat bones and place it lightly on top of your head (figure 3.14). Think about freeing your head and neck joint allowing your head to release upward, which will encourage the spine to lengthen.

Notice the extra space through the upper body and between the pelvis and rib cage. Do these changes alter the weight through your seat bones, the contact with your thighs on the chair, and your feet on the floor? Experiment in the chair with rocking forward and backward on your seat bones. Is this different from how you would normally lean forward, to work at a desk for example? You are now moving from your hip joints, so you should have a clear feedback from your seat bones. Remember that any *habit* patterns you detect on the ground will be exaggerated in the saddle.

Let us take a look at what happens when you sit on your horse. Sit in the lowest part of the saddle. Are you aware of your seat bones? They form your supporting base. Is your pelvis upright or tilting (figure 3.15)?

The muscles around the lower back and pelvis affect a rider's

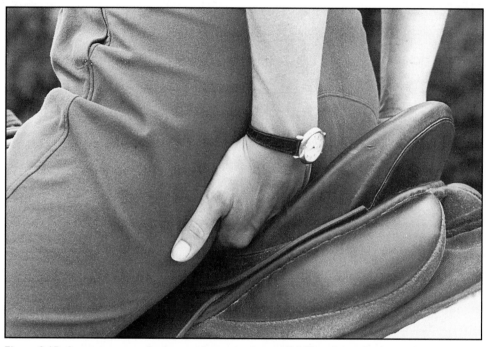

Figure 3.15 Are you aware of your seat bones in the saddle? They form the base of your support together with the muscles surrounding the pelvis. You need to be balanced over them to ride effectively.

ability to sit deep in the saddle. Try the following activity to help you loosen your hip joints and release the muscles through the lower back while keeping the upper body in balance. If your horse is quiet, cross your stirrups and ask someone to hold him while you put your knees over the front of the saddle. Take care not to clamp your thighs inward (figure 3.16). Make sure that you think of the connection from your seat bones to your head and vice versa. Ask your helper to notice if your upper body is aligned over your seat.

If your horse is safe and calm, ask your helper to lead you into a

Figure 3.16 Knees over the saddle on a very quiet horse! This is a good way of finding your seat bones if you are experiencing difficulties. Take care that you are also thinking of the space between each vertebra and that the neck muscles are released.

Figure 3.17 Making the same connection on a real horse as on the wooden one. Think of your neck being free before you think of your seat bones and the length of the spine.

walk. Be aware of the contact of your seat bones in the saddle. Does the contact differ from when your feet are in the stirrups? Are you contracting your stomach muscles? Observe your horse's shoulder movement and think of allowing each knee to release forward and away from your hip as the horse takes each shoulder forward. Do this in time with the steps. Can you feel how the horse's back moves your seat bones? Remember to keep thinking about the connection from your seat bones to the top of your head (figure 3.17). Once you have an increased awareness of your seat, ask your helper to take your legs and place them again in the riding position. Allow your legs to hang. Are they freer and are you sitting more deeply in the saddle? If the muscles through the thighs are contracted, your area of support will be narrowed.

Even when your seat bones are not in contact with the saddle, such as in the jumping position, the muscles surrounding the pelvis need to be elastic. If they are tight they hamper the rider's ability to hinge from the hips, flex in the knee, and absorb momentum through

Figure 3.18 Stand with your back against a wall, feet a little away from the wall but the pelvis still making contact with it. The head must be relaxed, not in contact with the wall.

the ankle joints. A similar position to that of jumping was devised by Alexander who called it the "position of mechanical advantage." It encourages a lengthening and widening of the back and freedom in the rib cage, with greater flexibility in the hips, knees, and ankle joints. The following activity will demonstrate this position.

Stand with your back against a wall, with your feet apart and your heels a few centimeters away from the baseboard. Make sure you do not pull your head back against the wall. Allow the wall to support you (figure 3.18).

Now slide a few centimeters down the wall by releasing your knees forward and directing them away from each other. Keep your feet flat on the floor. If the knees pull together or the lower back and pelvis come away from the wall, it usually means that there is excess tension in the lower back. You need to make sure you continue to direct the knees apart while keeping the lower back and pelvis in contact with the wall (figure 3.19).

Now lean forward by folding at the hip joint. Think of the head leading the body and be aware that your balance is being altered by the angle at the hip joint. Your weight should be evenly distributed over your feet. This is the "position of mechanical advantage." Some riders find that they have difficulty keeping the angle between the top of the thigh and the pelvis open enough to stay balanced (figure 3.20).

Stiffness will be highlighted when jumping if the rider folds from the waist instead of the hips. This interferes with the distribution of weight over the feet, because the rider is too far forward and the weight cannot be anchored down through to the heel. Too long a stirrup may well be the initial cause, because it causes the rider to reach for the stirrup with the toe instead of thinking about overall balance.

Figure 3.19 Now think of the knees releasing away from your hips. Make sure that you leave the pelvis in contact with the wall, and your feet flat on the ground. This will show up any stiffness in the hips, knees, and ankles.

Figure 3.20 Lean forward, bending at the hip joints. Notice how the weight transfers more onto the balls of your feet. If you ankles are stiff, you'll have difficulty keeping your heels flat on the ground. This is Alexander's "position of mechanical advantage."

Muscle Tone and Sensitivity

Full and accurate feedback from the rider's body relies on a healthy muscle tone, which can only be maintained by consistent *good use*. Now that you have become familiar with your joints, let's look at the muscles that hold them together.

How Muscles Work

A healthy muscle is one that is able to contract and then release back to its normal resting state. Unfortunately, the muscles of many riders are less elastic than they need to be because of excessive effort and tension routinely used in everyday life. As certain muscles become habitually over-shortened and stiff, the opposing ones may become over-lengthened. The resulting imbalance of the musculature is ultimately responsible for pulling the body gradually out of alignment. Muscles that are constantly tense will cause joint surfaces to compress and important sensory feedback will be limited and distorted. In addition, postural support is disturbed and balancing skills are reduced.

How Muscles are Linked to the Brain

Muscle fibers contract in response to nerve signals from the brain and spinal cord. The final signal is carried through motor nerves, which make direct contact with the muscles. In the ideal situation, the spinal cord and brain are continuously informed of what all the muscles are doing, of their degree of tension, and of their speed of contraction or relaxation. This feedback from the musculature and the joints is essential for a smooth, coordinated performance. The feedback information arises in sensory organelles within the muscles, called muscle spindles and tendon organs. The spindles are continuously influenced by their own motor nerve supply, which adjusts their sensitivity according to the needs of the moment.

Over-shortening of muscles due to excessive effort interferes both with the responsiveness and elasticity of those muscles and with the performance of their muscle spindles. This means that riders who are tense are reducing the sensory information available to them. Their ability to communicate with the horse will be impaired and they will have little chance of improving their "*sense of feel*" — the ability to feel what is happening to their own bodies and their horses.

Muscle Tone

The basis for a well-developed *sense of feel* lies in an even distribution of muscle tone throughout the body. A good rider uses minimum muscular effort, and yet her muscles are well toned. There is great misunderstanding as to what constitutes good muscle tone, which is a combination of strength with sensitivity and elasticity. Riders do not require the same muscular strength as a hurdler or marathon runner. If muscles are over-developed or consistently contracted over a period of time they become desensitised, while others that are under-used become flaccid. Riders who are either too rigid or too relaxed will lose sensitivity and control. One of the goals of the BodySense courses is to use the Alexander Technique to find and maintain appropriate muscle tone without losing sensitivity and elasticity.

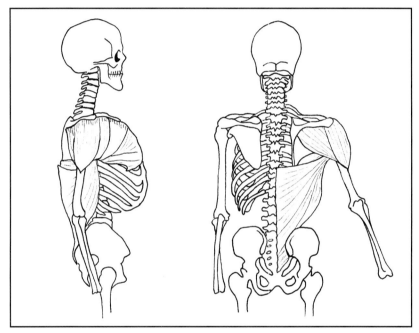

Figure 3.21 Notice how muscles that surround the rib cage also attach to the arms and back. You can see how tension in the shoulders affects breathing capacity.

Breathing

Another important and much neglected part of our lives and our riding is correct breathing. Few riders are aware that their breathing affects their back muscles and can interfere with balance and coordination. The way you breathe will affect your ability to sit deeply in the saddle. Holding your breath creates tension and tightens the muscles that surround the diaphragm and pelvis, thus causing the seat to lift, which narrows your base of support. In addition, if you are breathing inefficiently, (most people do), all the muscles surrounding your breathing apparatus become contracted and your lung capacity is reduced (figures 3.21 & 3.22). Try the following activity to assess your breathing efficiency.

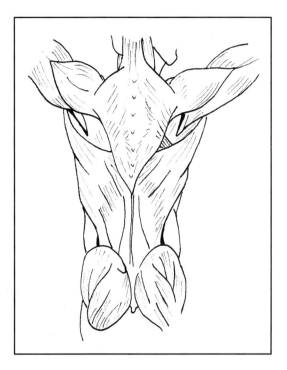

Figure 3.22 The muscles around the sides of the body interconnect with the muscles of the neck and shoulders. If any of these muscles are constricted, they deprive the back of elasticity.

Figure 3.23 Hands on the ribs, think of allowing the ribs to move and expand sideways, rather than pulling upward.

Sit at a table in front of a lighted candle. Keeping your lips relaxed, blow out gently so the flame flickers but is not extinguished. Now wait and see what happens to your breath. Do you draw the air back in? Blow out again and trust that the air will come back in without conscious effort. Most riders are unaware that they suck or gasp air back in. Blow out again. This time placing your hands lightly on your lower ribs (figure 3.23).

As you softly blow the air out, the ribs should be drawn inward. If you can consciously wait to allow air to come in again, you will notice how the ribs expand sideways (the amount will vary according to how much flexibility you have in this area). The back should also be widened. Resist the temptation to pull upward with the chest since this will lessen the freedom in the lower ribs.

How does this apply to riding? The next time you ride a transition, think of allowing the air to flow out as you are applying your aid. This will benefit the quality of the transition since your seat will be in greater contact with the saddle so your horse will get a clearer message.

The "Whispered Ah" Procedure

F.M. Alexander used to measure his pupils' coordination by the quality and regularity of their breathing. He devised a procedure to help students discover how they were interfering with their breathing. When done correctly, Alexander used to say that this procedure, called the "*whispered ah*" was a tonic for the whole system.

Use a mirror or, better still, ask your Alexander teacher to help you. Place two fingers on your jaw joint and let the lower jaw drop. Notice whether you tend to take your head back or drop your face downward as you do this. The jaw movement should be as independent from other motion as possible. Observe where your jaw hinges, then take your fingers away from your jaw. Now, with your lips closed, take your tongue to the roof of your mouth and feel where the soft palate is situated. Allow your tongue to relax. Repeat the tongue motion with your hand on the front of your neck: do you feel movement in the muscles? Now place the tip of your tongue gently behind the lower teeth. Think of smiling with the muscles that are situated underneath your eyes. Keep the sensation of widening your face muscles as you drop your lower jaw. Be careful that you do not take your head backward or forward and that you keep your mouth open. Think of the roof of the mouth as a dome shape and the back of the throat as a cave as you allow the air to come out on a "*whispered ah*" sound (figure 3.24). Do not gasp air in, just let whatever air is in your lungs expel slowly. Now close your mouth and let the air come in through your

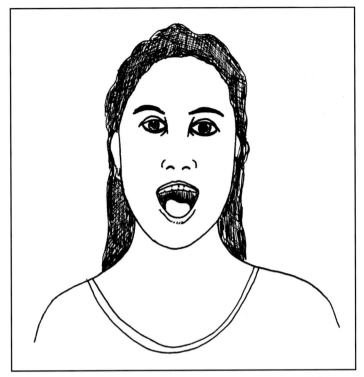

Figure 3.24 The "whispered ah" encourages greater awareness of breathing and demonstrates how bad habits like gasping in air hamper lung capacity. The problem with most people is that they do not get rid of air efficiently.

nose without gasping. Do not vocalise the "ah," if you hear a grating or rasping sound, this usually means that the back of the throat is not sufficiently open.

When riding, "*whispered ahs*" put you in touch with the lower back since muscles surrounding the back of the diaphragm are rooted in the lower back and affect the weight on the seat bones. You can also learn to synchronise your breathing with your horse, which helps build greater rapport between the two of you. Breathing is also very important in maintaining poise, which you will learn more about in Chapter Five.

Vision

In the book *Centered Riding,* Sally Swift refers to "hard" and "soft" eyes. By hard eyes she means that you "look intently at an object, concentrating on its exact outlines, shape, density, and color."[10] Riders often look intently at their horses' ears with hard eyes, which tends to block out sensitivity in the body. Soft eyes, on the other hand, allow an object to be central to your vision but you are also aware of the area above, below and surrounding it, which means you are then using your peripheral vision. "The more area you encompass with the eyes the more you'll be aware of your seat. Using soft eyes is like a new philosophy. It's a method of becoming distinctly aware of what is going on around you, beneath you, and inside you."[11]

Research has shown that the quality of vision can be linked to state of mind. When a person is awake, there are two brainwave frequencies, "alpha" and "beta." If a rider is anxious, the faster beta waves tend to become activated, causing "hard eyes," narrowed vision, and excess tension, resulting in a loss of harmony with the horse. Unfortunately, anxiety causes actions to become hurried, so that mind and body no longer work together and there is a loss of awareness of self, a phenomenon many riders have experienced. On the other hand, when the mind is calm but receptive — when alpha waves are present — the chances of gaining poise and a good rapport between horse and rider are greatly increased. It is thought that alpha waves also help to free the mind from doubts and negative emotions, and that they enhance creativity. The eyes could be said to be "soft" when alpha waves are present.

Try this experiment to see how far your vision extends and to enhance your peripheral vision, which encourages alpha brainwaves. You will need a partner. Sit in a chair with your partner standing beside it. Ask your partner to place her index finger approximately nine inches in front of your eyes. Keep your eyes on the finger as she slowly moves her finger to the side of your face and gradually around toward the back of your head (figure 3.25).

Follow with your eyes but do not move your head or shoulders. Tell your partner to stop at the point at which her finger disappears. Now let the eyes lead the head to look at the finger. Then look in front of you again. Do this to the left and the right. Is there a difference in your vision either way or does your head move more easily to one side than the other?

Now repeat the experiment, but this time when the finger disappears think about freeing your neck and turning your head from your *atlanto-occipital joint* (see page 7, figure 1.7). Is there now a difference in the amount of movement and quality of your peripheral vision when you use this joint? Many riders find that there is a marked improvement. Take the time to stop and think before moving (figure 3.26).

Figure 3.25 When experimenting with peripheral vision, "eyes in the back of your head" takes on a new meaning. Follow the finger without moving your head.

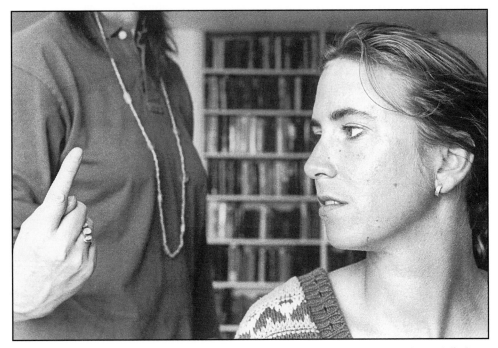

Figure 3.26 Now think of freeing the neck before you turn your head — tension in the neck limits your vision.

Balance

"To be a good rider you must stay on the horse through the erectness and balance of the trunk."
Basic Equitation, Commandant Jean Licart of the Cadre Noir.[12]

Many riders become focused on their seat only, when it is the correct overall balance of the upper body that is crucial. Imagine the following scene:

All eyes are fixed on a tightrope walker poised fifty feet above the ground. She is balancing precariously halfway across the wire, and as she pauses to adjust her balance everyone holds their breath. There is no safety net. The walker first raises her arms and then flexes her knees to lower her center of gravity. Her knees and feet quiver as she adjusts her equilibrium. Too much tension would cause her to stiffen and overbalance, too little and she will collapse and fall over.

Riding a horse is also a balancing act albeit not so dramatic as the high wire. "Following the horse's movements is inevitably connected with flexibility and feeling: there is no room for stiffness or rigidity, for brute strength or great activity." *Riding Logic,* Wilhelm Müseler.[13] A good proportion of riding ability can be attributed to balance. But have you ever considered what is meant by being in balance (figure 3.27)?

The ideal riding position is one in which an imaginary line can be drawn from the back of the ear through the elbow, to the hip and

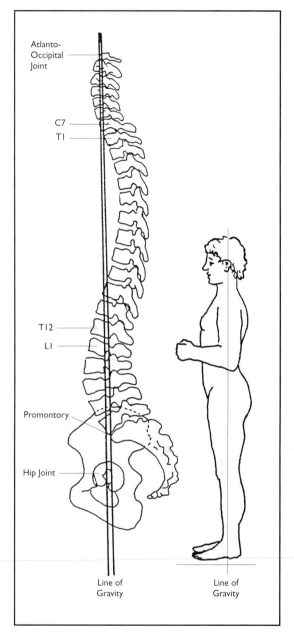

Figure 3.27 Bodyweight is distributed more or less evenly in front and back of the line of gravity. Good balance is based on the relationship of the head-neck-spine-hip to the line of gravity.

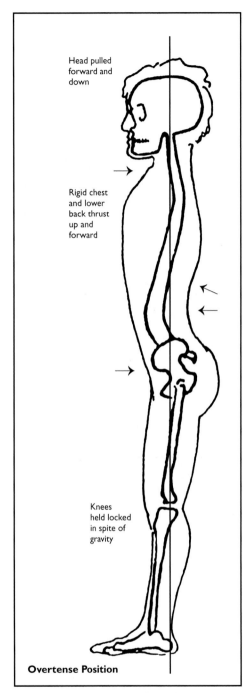

Head pulled
forward and
down

Rigid chest
and lower
back thrust
up and
forward

Knees
held locked
in spite of
gravity

Overtense Position

Figure 3.28 Different standing *habits* — note the approach of the body as a whole to the line of gravity.

heel. This line is used as a goal to encourage riders to be as close as possible to the line of their center of gravity, thereby achieving optimum balance. To do this well, the rider's body needs to be supple. Just as a horse with a fixed outline lacks fluidity, so a rider who fixes her position causes her body to become rigid and incapable of accommodating the horse's rhythm and movement. Good trainers would not dream of forcing their horses into a shape that robs them of freedom and suppleness. Why should a rider do to herself what she wouldn't do to her horse (figure 3.28)?

Balance needs only minimum muscular effort, but maintaining a balanced upright position requires continuous thought and awareness, and it is this skill that has to be learned and practised. Better balance generally evolves from a release of excess tension, which then allows the body to adopt its natural shape. Capable riders not only balance themselves, but their horses, too. Their posture is achieved through suppleness and poise rather than tension or grip. They have tone throughout their bodies with the weight evenly distributed on both seat bones. The arms and legs hang independently and the rider can absorb the horse's movement through her back, seat, and hips. This requires a connection from the head, neck, and back to the sitting bones. If this coordination is incomplete, the back becomes disengaged and the arms and legs will then compensate by tightening to keep the rider from falling off. She may well end up either behind or in front of her true center of gravity. Lets look at an example of how this happens.

Figure 3.29
Jayne experiences tremendous muscle tension in the saddle. Notice how her neck muscles are contracting, causing her back to compress and balance to come way behind the line of gravity. The distribution of Jayne's weight has culminated over her coccyx (tail bone). She will be unable to absorb movement in her back muscles and will have to resort to gripping with her legs to stay in the saddle.

Case History

Jayne was having difficulty going with her horse's movement. She found that she was often left behind if her horse quickened his step or made an upward transition, for instance from the walk to the trot. "I feel as if my body is always trying to catch up with my horse." Jayne was unaware how much she was contracting her stomach muscles and sitting on the back of her seat bones (figure 3.29). This meant that to stay upright in the saddle she gripped excessively with her thighs and thus blocked the movement in her hips. Jayne's lower back and neck muscles were rigid with tension and in order to balance she had to brace her upper body backward. Not surprisingly, she was also holding herself in a similar pattern when sitting or standing on the ground (figure 3.30). As a result of her BodySense course, Jayne's body became more aligned through the release of unnecessary tension. Once Jayne learned to

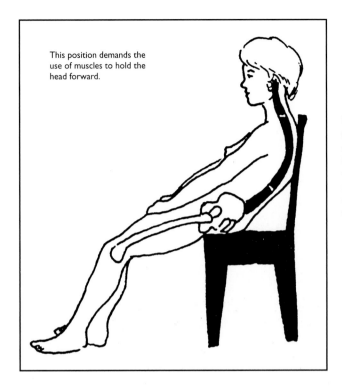

This position demands the use of muscles to hold the head forward.

Figure 3.30 Jayne also exhibits similar posture sitting on a chair. Notice how she has to use her neck and shoulder muscles to hold herself up. The back muscles are slack and it will be difficult for her to engage them when she is sitting on a horse.

stop over-contracting some of her muscles, she could stay in harmony with her horse.

Case History

Anita often found that she was in front of her horse's movement. She poked her head forward and rounded her shoulders; like Jayne her stomach muscles as well as those surrounding her pelvis and thighs were tight. As she tipped forward with her upper body, her lower legs came back and her legs caused the horse to shoot off when she gave an aid. Anita stood on the ground with her head jutting forward and her shoulders were hunched. Her pelvis and legs were fixed and her knees were braced back. As a result she was not properly balanced over her feet.

After ten or so Alexander sessions, Anita had become more aware of how she was upsetting her balance. This helped enormously when she sat in the saddle during her BodySense course, and she was able to stop getting in front of her horse's movement as her balance improved.

These two examples illustrate the difficulties riders face when the coordination through the head, neck, and back (*primary control*) is not functioning. Just as a horse uses more effort and moves inefficiently when its back is not engaged, so a similar *misuse* occurs in people.

Riding Styles

Although the rider's position in the saddle is somewhat different in various riding styles, balance and harmony with the horse is always the goal. The rider must remain in the center of gravity, regardless of the stirrup length (figure 3.31).

Figure 3.31 Whether you're jumping or not, flexibility in the hip joint is imperative for all riding disciplines. Riders often get confused as to where they should fold or bend, especially while jumping; the bend should be from the hip, as in the photo, not from the waist.

Racing

Even though jockeys ride in the most forward seat of all, they need to be neither too high nor too far forward, because this will burden the horse's forehand (figure 3.32).

> *"A jockey must be able to recognise at all moments the muscular tension, the state of balance and the reserves of energy of his horse to judge the moment to start the race to the finish and, while preserving his feeling for strength, speed and stride, he must also watch the opposition — and all this happens in a matter of seconds"*
> from *The Way to Perfect Horsemanship* by Udo Bürger.[14]

Figure 3.32 Notice how both horse and jockey display poise even after finishing a race. There is a sense of forwardness in the horse as it is well connected through his back. The jockey exudes an upwardness through his body despite the difficulties imposed by the jockey position (very short stirrups and balance forward of the center of gravity when in motion). It would be all too easy for the jockey to scrunch down into himself but instead he appears very light.

Show Jumping

The length of stirrup used in show jumping varies according to the height of the rider and the size of fences involved. If the rider perpetually swings more to one side than the other while in the air, the horse has to shift his balance the other way to compensate. If the rider is left behind the movement over the fence the horse will get jabbed in the mouth. If she is in front of the movement, the horse finds it difficult to take off and land easily because the forelegs are overloaded.

For both show jumping and cross-country riding, the rider needs to be in such a secure position that the knee and ankle joints can absorb stress from above and below, which means that the hip joints need to be equally supple. A good position allows more weight to be taken through the lower legs, which must be close to the horse's sides. The rider's hands can then follow the movement of the horse's head and neck as they stretch forward over the jump.

Cross-Country Jumping

Cross-country jumping takes place over varied terrain, and solid obstacles are jumped at speed, so there is little room for error. Although the extra speed gives impetus, which allows for a greater range of take-off points than in show jumping, any defects in training become intensified at faster paces. The rider needs to keep the horse balanced and in rhythm at all times, taking into account the state of the ground, severity of the fences, and her horse's experience as well as her own. A rider who has a stable position plays a large part in the horse's ability to regain his balance after a jump (figures 3.33 & 3.34). The rider must be ready to adapt her position to different types of fences — drop, uphill, water, oxer — so as not to cause the horse to hit the fence or fall (figure 3.35).

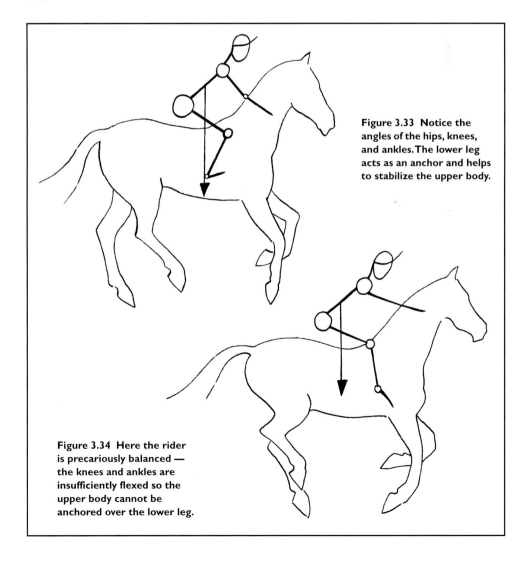

Figure 3.33 **Notice the angles of the hips, knees, and ankles. The lower leg acts as an anchor and helps to stabilize the upper body.**

Figure 3.34 **Here the rider is precariously balanced — the knees and ankles are insufficiently flexed so the upper body cannot be anchored over the lower leg.**

Figure 3.35 Minette Rice-Edwards and Fisherman over a spread at the Badminton Three-Day Event.

Consequence of Bad Habits

The balance of horse and rider can easily be disturbed when the rider does not recognise that she has developed a bad *habit*. Let's look at the common problem of a rider sitting crooked in the saddle. Crookedness in the rider is often a result of a tendency to *misuse* the body in daily life. It develops from using one side of the body more than the other, which causes a twist. The predominant side becomes more muscularly developed and stronger. The other side is less muscle bound and therefore freer, but weaker and used less. If a rider is not aware of this imbalance on the ground, she will be constantly using and therefore strengthening, the stronger side while neglecting the weaker, making it virtually impossible to change in the saddle. A rider needs to be aware that what feels comfortable and familiar may actually be reinforcing bad *habits*, just as a horse that is allowed to work with his body crookedly will develop uneven muscles on each side of his body (figure 3.36).

Attempting to change the shape or outline by putting the body in a correct position will not affect the *habit* behind the *misuse*. As Alexander said, "Change involves carrying out an activity against the habit of life."[15] It is the *habit* that must be changed.

Figure 3.36 The rider has collapsed her right hip, which has thrown her weight onto the left hip and affected the weight distribution through the entire right-hand side of her body — the shoulder, ribcage, and forearms, as well as the pelvis.

Most teaching methods rely on imitation and repetition to achieve the desired result. Riding instructors seek to show "how it should be done" and their pupils are encouraged to imitate them as best they can. Attention is focused on gaining the end result — *endgaining*. There is little regard for the processes involved in achieving it. Mistakes that are consistently repeated in attempts to "get it right" unconsciously become part of the pupil's repertoire. Instructors and students assume that these can be corrected and ironed out as the overall performance improves. However, this is easier said than done and it ignores the power of *habit*.

The Alexander Technique offers a different method of learning. It teaches pupils to focus on the *means whereby* — a process of thinking, and potentially being, in a state of readiness, thus avoiding the habitual pitfalls before they occur. An Alexander teacher can see a

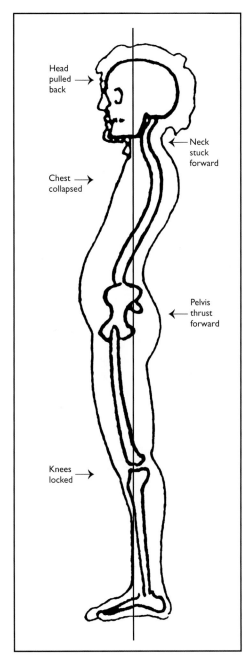

Figure 3.37 Neil's manner of standing on the ground.

Head pulled back →

Chest collapsed →

← Neck stuck forward

← Pelvis thrust forward

Knees locked →

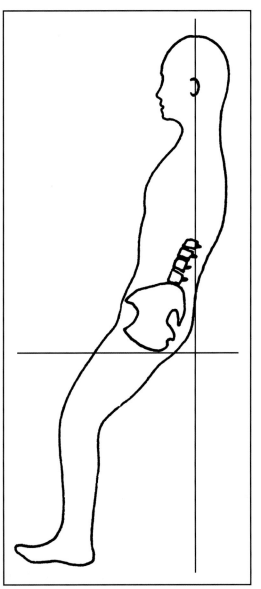

Figure 3.38 Only gripping with the legs will keep this rider from falling off due to lack of upright balance. Can you guess where most of the tension is going to be distributed? The muscles surrounding the pelvis and thighs; the stomach and ribs also will be constricted.

rider's weaknesses as she sits in a chair and knows how these are likely to be exacerbated in the saddle.

The correct balance of the body in the saddle requires mind and body interaction. This coordination will not be automatically accessible to the rider unless it is used in everyday life.

Case History

Many riders try to force themselves into the "correct" position. This creates further *misuse* and interferes with overall balance and coordination. Over a period of time, the effort of holding the body with that excessive tension can cause damage that leads to pain and injury.

Neil, a novice rider, took up lessons in the Alexander Technique to help with pain in his hip. During riding lessons he had been trying hard, "to get his legs further back underneath him." In his fourth riding lesson he used such force that he damaged the muscles surrounding his hip joint. After several weeks rest, Neil attempted to ride again. He was extremely disappointed to find that sitting in the saddle for any length of time made the pain worse. During his first Alexander lesson, Neil was shown how he was already tightening and fixing his hip joints before getting on the horse by throwing his pelvis forward, which tipped his upper body back (figures 3.37 & 3.38).

To stand upright, Neil braced his legs by locking the knees, which hollowed his lower back. This holding and bracing created a stiffness that was reflected in his walking. Over a period of time, moving in this manner had diminished the mobility in his hip joints. Neil's problem is very common, and it was highlighted when he rode because he did not have the required degree of flexibility in the hips to attain a good position.

Since his injury, Neil had created a postural imbalance by putting more weight on to his good hip to compensate for the pain in the other one. As he became aware of this he corrected the *habit* and the pain diminished. He could then move with greater freedom, especially through his hip joints. The patterns of holding and stiffening had less and less influence over him. BodySense courses are designed to help people with problems such as Neil's to carry out the philosophies of the Alexander Technique while in the saddle.

Case History

Emily is a keen combined training rider who had several back injuries over a number of years. She had ignored the pain until it became bad enough to force her to seek help. She could not sit or walk for long, let alone ride. Emily works in an office but had previously been a model.

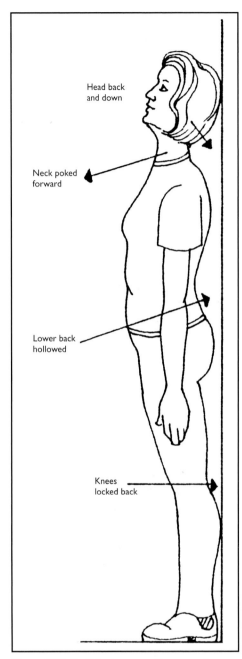

Head back
and down

Neck poked
forward

Lower back
hollowed

Knees
locked back

Figure 3.39 Emily's stance on the ground.

She had become expert at swinging her pelvis as she walked, which put pressure on her lower back and disturbed her balance. Emily's neck muscles were over-contracted, pulling her head down onto her spine and compressing the disks between the vertebrae (figures 3.39 & 3.40). After several weeks of lessons, she began to release the tension in her neck, which significantly reduced the downward pressure on her back. She also learned that she did not need the excessive swing of her hips to walk. She was delighted to find herself pain free and was able to return to work.

A week or so later, she came in for her regular Alexander lesson looking dejected, drawn, and tired. The pain had returned and she was at a loss to explain why. As the lesson progressed the pain began to ease. She realised that she had fallen back into her old *habit* pattern because she had tried to do too much too quickly. Just as horses need time to establish changes in their training, so humans need time to consolidate similar progress made in Alexander lessons. New patterns of coordination can be easily overridden by the strength of the old ones. After approximately ten weeks, Emily was sufficiently pain free to try riding again, and BodySense teaching helped to further consolidate the *good use* she had been taught. At first Emily's new coordination felt strange and unfamiliar, but as long as she paid attention to it, she strained less and she remained pain free.

Emily is now riding regularly again. She says "My riding has improved no end. I feel more in balance with my horse. BodySense has taught me how to use my back correctly. This has given me greater stability and a more solid foundation to work from. I feel that I am no longer being pulled out of the saddle and I have the horse more

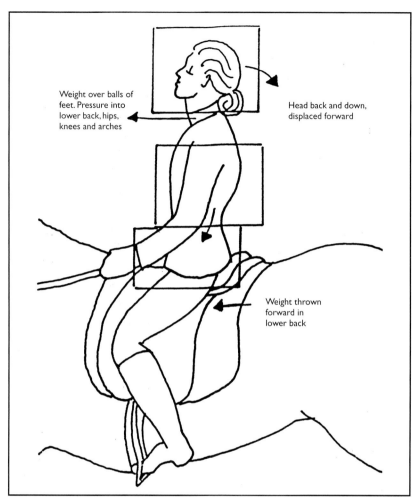

Weight over balls of
feet. Pressure into
lower back, hips,
knees and arches

Head back and down,
displaced forward

Weight thrown
forward in
lower back

Figure 3.40 Emily in the saddle.

underneath me. If I went back to riding in my old way, the pain in my
back returned instantly. When I corrected my position, it was immediately alleviated."

Emily had experienced the link between her pain and her habitual *misuse*. By applying what she had learned in her Alexander and
BodySense lessons, she could stop the old pattern of muscular tension
from recurring. Emily's case demonstrates the power of *habits* and the
harmful effects they can produce if they are left unchecked.

Learning BodySense is like setting out on a journey. You need to
be motivated and prepared to observe yourself and not be afraid to
experiment. Allowing yourself to learn from your mistakes reduces
tension and counteracts habitual responses. If you accept that you do
not have to be right the first time and that it is possible to benefit from
a mistake, then you are well on the way to enjoying the learning process.

4

Ride with BodySense

The Limitations of Verbal Instruction

The way you react to instructions has a profound effect on the mind and body. "Head up, shoulders back, heels down," your instructor repeats patiently for what seems like the umpteenth time. This time you try even harder to get it right, yet the harder you try, the more your body tenses up and fails to respond in the way you wish. It is as if there were a missing link between your brain and your body that seems to render you incapable of carrying out your instructor's wishes! Does this sound all too familiar? Like many riding instructors, Alexander realised that the majority of his pupils struggled to carry out his instructions, not because they did not try hard enough, but because they were greatly affected by his choice of words and their interpretation. He got around this problem by developing a special use of his hands to overcome the limitations of verbal instructions. This continues to be an important aspect of the Alexander Technique, teaching riders a *sense of feel*.

The Rider's Sense of Feel

"Good feel" is essential for enhancing a horse's way of going. Feel is an ability to know the precise strength and timing of the aids needed for each different horse. A rider may have a correct position and be well balanced, but unless her *sense of feel* is well developed, she will always be at a disadvantage. With good feel a rider has that extra edge to monitor and influence the quality of the horse's movement.

Instruction cannot teach the true meaning of feel, because it is an experience based on the rider's ability to interpret information via the senses. This ability is limited when the rider is not sensitive enough to be aware of minute changes in balance, speed, and rhythm. For example, she may not be able to notice when her horse varies his rhythm or alters his stride, or she may not be able to regulate the size of his steps. In addition, the rider may not interpret correctly the information coming from her own body. For instance, she may feel that her lower leg is on the girth when actually it is too far forward.

Do these examples mean that the above pupils are inherently insensitive and therefore will never be good riders? No, it does not. Other riders may appear to have feel but they do not have the control or coordination to carry out instructions. There can be a discrepancy between what the rider feels and what the instructor sees. Failure to interpret information from the body correctly leads riders into great difficulties. Good feel is often assumed to be the sole prerogative of talented riders, while many instructors acknowledge that they cannot teach it. It is, however, possible to improve feel and develop its various qualities in the BodySense courses.

Humans process information about themselves and their environment through the five senses of sight, hearing, smell, taste, and touch. Yet none of these really incorporates the rider's *sense of feel*. It is the *kinesthetic* sense, which is an important element of body awareness that incorporates movement.

To discover this sense in yourself, put a hand up above your head for a moment and wiggle your fingers without looking at them. Your *kinesthetic* sense gives you an impression of the position and shape of your hand in space, the speed with which you are wiggling your fingers, the amount of tension you are using to do it, and the distance each finger is from the others. Notice that if you now look at your hand, still above your head, the information from the *kinesthetic* sense tends to fade into the background. The *kinesthetic* sense is sometimes described as the lost sixth sense. It is this *kinesthetic* or movement sense that helps monitor crucial factors such as how the horse is going, how the rider is positioned in the saddle, and the degree of effort needed to execute the aids. It is important for riders to acknowledge this sense and know that it can be developed through training.

Understanding the Kinesthetic Sense
The *kinesthetic* sense monitors tension through receptors in the joints, muscles, and tendons, which then is passed back to the brain. The brain is incapable of absorbing and processing all the information available at the same time. It filters and selects a small proportion of the most interesting and relevant information at any one moment. Knowl-

edge that is new or indicates danger tends to take precedence over that which is constantly present. For example, on a busy road a rider is more likely to be attending to outside information that tells her which direction her horse is taking than in detailed information about her position in the saddle. If a rider has a horse that requires that her awareness remain concerned with what the horse is doing all the time, then self-awareness is habitually diminished and access to the *kinesthetic* sense is impeded. This sense can also be blocked by excess tension, which causes the muscles surrounding the joints to tighten up thus restricting the flow of sensory information from the receptors. No amount of attention to the horse will help the rider to regain sensitivity and awareness. The correction lies within the rider, not the horse.

Sensitivity

Sensory information from the body is always present. It becomes so familiar that it tends to be pushed into the background in favour of more stimulating external information. Humans generally rely to a large extent on the visual sense to orientate themselves in the environment. A blind person, however, will learn to rely on hearing and touch. Each sense can be heightened by increased consciousness of its input. An artist tends to have a more sophisticated eye for detail than the average person; the musician, a greater auditory sensitivity; and the wine taster, a more refined sense of taste. A dancer, of course, would have an increased awareness of the *kinesthetic* sense. Different people favour particular areas of sensory information. Both *kinesthetic* and visual senses need to be developed and integrated for optimum balance. Each rider's *sense of feel* will vary and be unique to them because it is a matter of individual awareness and experience.

Sensory Deception

Sensory awareness can become distorted. To assess whether your *kinesthetic* sense is accurate, try the following activity.

Put both your arms out in front of you, palms facing downward, and position them so that they are horizontal and parallel. Close your eyes and take the right arm up forty-five degrees and take the left arm down forty-five degrees. Keeping your eyes closed, bring the arms back to the horizontal so that they are parallel again. Open your eyes and look at the position of your arms. Are they parallel? If not, adjust them and notice the sensory feedback.

You can try another experiment to test the position of your limbs in space. Close your eyes and place your feet so that they feel parallel,

Figure 4.1 But, I couldn't possibly feel more upright!

approximately one foot apart and underneath your hips. Open your eyes and notice the actual position of your feet. Does it match with your sensing of the position? If not, alter the position so that your feet are parallel and notice how that feels.

The results of these experiments often show a discrepancy between what feels right through the *kinesthetic* sense and what is reality. An example from Alexander's writings highlights this common discrepancy. He worked with a little crippled girl whose body was extremely twisted and contorted, and was able to reduce the twist significantly. However, after he had finished working with her, the child felt that she had been pulled out of shape. She thought she was even more crooked, when in fact she was straighter. This is an example of what Alexander called faulty "*sensory appreciation*" by which riders can be hampered to a greater or lesser extent. For example, a rider who is used to leaning forward, will often report that it feels as if she is leaning backward when in fact she has been shown an upright position. This indicates the hazards of relying on the *kinesthetic* sense for assessing a correct position! (figure 4.1).

Alexander's contribution to the riding world is the development of a technique to consciously improve the "*use* of the self." The more a rider can improve her standard of *use* of herself, the more accurate and sensitive her *kinesthetic* sense becomes. This is not achieved by setting out directly to train the *kinesthetic* sense through deliberate exercises, but instead an indirect approach that links mind and body and ultimately leads to more accurate sensory feedback.

The Independent Seat

Most riders acknowledge the need to gain an independent seat, but few understand the true meaning of this term (figure 4.2). It means that the rider can sit in the deepest part of the saddle without relying on her arms or legs to stay upright. She is balanced and in self-carriage, so that whatever movement the horse makes she can remain with him.

Figure 4.2 A truly independent seat: Nuno Oliveira

One of the best places to look for an example of an independent seat is the Spanish Riding School of Vienna. Anyone who has ever seen their performance knows that the riders are elegantly poised and in perfect harmony with their horses. Even when the horses perform the "Airs Above the Ground," where horses literally leap into the air, the riders appear to be glued to the saddle. Such skill takes years of work and dedication. To gain it, pupils at the Spanish Riding School spend time on the longe line daily for three years, until an independent seat is achieved. Even advanced riders go back on the longe from time to time, to prevent bad *habits* from creeping back.

Alois Podhajsky, former Director of the Spanish Riding School, has said that "The training of the rider commences with the teaching of the correct seat, which is the basic requirement for any kind of riding, especially dressage. The rider's seat must be supple and flexible, upright and deep in order to give the correct aids without disturbing the balance of the horse, especially in difficult exercises."[16]

Few riders are able to spend the necessary time and money to develop a truly independent seat, yet without one they diminish the horse's ability to progress, as well as their own safety, comfort, and true potential.

To apply the aids effectively and in harmony with the horse's movement, the rider must have delicate, precise control of her limbs. A rider with an independent seat is conscious of and capable of regulating the amount of effort needed by each limb so that the aids can be applied without force. To give a leg aid, one needs only a small movement of the lower leg involving flexion of the knee joint, while the rest of the body, undisturbed, continues to be in balance and in rhythm with the horse (figures 4.3 & 4.4).

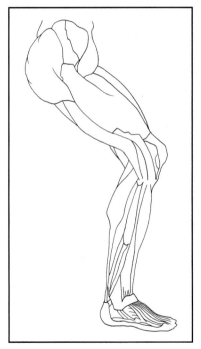

Figure 4.3 Outer aspect of the leg: notice how the muscles from the pelvis connect with the leg muscles.

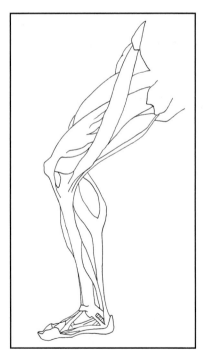

Figure 4.4 Inner aspect of the leg: you can see how tension in any of the muscles surrounding leg joints (hip, knee, and ankle) affects the others and how tightness in any part of the leg will affect the quality of the aids.

The essential concept of the independent seat is that for each limb to function freely, it requires understanding, knowledge, and above all, the experience of how all the limbs are connected to the body. Such body awareness is usually innate in talented riders, however, all riders can acquire this awareness with the help of BodySense, thereby improving their riding and enhancing the relationship with the horse. Once an independent seat is established, the aids can be applied efficiently.

Communicating with Your Horse: The Aids

Most riders apply the aids without synchronising with their horse's movement. If the horse doesn't respond immediately, they try harder by exerting more effort with the arms, legs, and seat, thus reducing the art of riding to a mechanical level. Such an approach is similar to someone in a foreign country whom, instead of learning the local language, expects to be understood by shouting louder in their own language! Using the aids more strongly fails to recognise that a touch on the horse's mouth or sides has registered in the horse's nervous system. Riders should heed the words of the great Nuno Oliveira, "to practice equestrian art is to establish a conversation on a higher level with the horse: a dialogue of courtesy and finesse." [17] The horse is not a machine, and the rider must learn to observe the speed of his responses, which will vary according to the horse's level of training, temperament, and conformation and the skill of the rider to interpret the horse's reactions.

Riders must have patience with a young horse, allowing him time to understand and react as required. As his level of training improves, the aids can become more and more subtle. Ultimately, little more than a thought is enough communication to achieve the desired result.

At all levels, the rider must have awareness and control over her body before she can apply the aids competently. Sadly, the way aids are often conveyed has a hindering effect on the horse. Aids have to be transmitted through the rider's body. The clarity and effectiveness of the message is therefore determined by how well the rider uses herself in the giving of these aids. This can be compared with the way an Alexander teacher uses her hands to guide her pupil during an Alexander lesson. The more attention the teacher or rider pays to the quality of their own coordination at the same time as giving the appropriate instruction or direction, the more clearly it will be received by the pupil or horse. The aids must stimulate the horse's mental processes. Too much effort creates excess tension, which interrupts communication. The principle is always more thought, less "doing."

For example, if the rider is tightening the leg in order to apply the aid, the message will be lacking in clarity. The problem is that most riders do not know what lightness in the leg means because they never experience it. The ability to allow the leg to hang freely from the hip joint can only occur if the whole body is in balance. If the upper body is unbalanced, the rider has no alternative but to grip with the leg to stay in the saddle. If the thigh is tight, it creates a lack of freedom in the muscles surrounding the pelvis and a rider who tightens these muscles while applying the leg is giving the horse a double message — stop from the pelvis and go forward from the leg. No wonder many sensitive horses become confused.

Using the aids intelligently is much more than a question of creating impulsion with the legs and controlling it with the hands. As the rider becomes more educated, she will learn to apply the aids by regulating and combining the intensity of pressure of legs, seat, and hands. When she can do this in time with the horse's movement, she can influence and enhance his way of going.

As Alois Podhajsky of the Spanish Riding School says: "But there is one principle that should never be abandoned, namely, that the rider must learn to control himself before he can control his horse. This is the basic, most important principle to be preserved in equitation."[18]

Using the Back

A rider who lacks connection in her own back is unable to influence her horse to gain engagement from his hindquarters, which is essential for true collection and lightness. Nuno Oliveira (see figure 4.2, page 69) was famous for consistently producing some of the best-collected and lightest horses in the world. He sat very erect with a strong but elastic back that is very different from many riders in current international dressage competitions, where some riders appear to be "driving" their horses with an exaggerated tilt of the pelvis (figure 4.5). Fortunately, most of the big warmbloods used in competitions can tolerate this amount of pressure on their backs, but less robust horses need riding with greater sensitivity (figure 4.6).

The term "bracing the back" has caused many misconceptions. "The action of the back, which riders describe as bracing the back, is brought about when the rider modifies the texture of his spine. He does so by altering the stretch and tension that runs through the spine, and by giving the spine a particular direction. The bracing of the back is sometimes accompanied by a subtle displacement of the rider's centre of gravity."[19]

By changing the tension in her lower back muscles, the rider

Figure 4.5 Tilting the pelvis and driving with the small of the back pulls riders out of balance and encourages the horse to hollow his back.

Figure 4.6 Daniel Pevsner, FBHS, as a pupil at the Spanish Riding School, sitting beautifully in balance and using his back correctly.

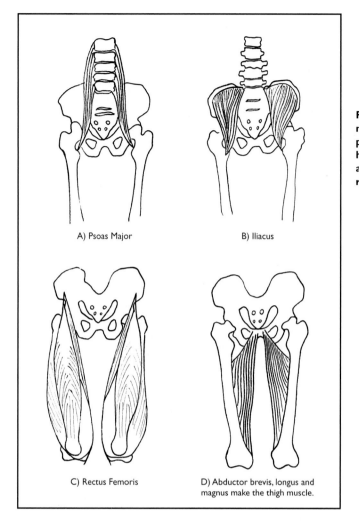

A) Psoas Major

B) Iliacus

C) Rectus Femoris

D) Abductor brevis, longus and magnus make the thigh muscle.

Figure 4.7 The four main muscles that attach the pelvis to the hips and the hips to the knees. Tension in any of these areas affects a rider's ability to sit deeply.

encourages the horse to collect and lighten his forehand. To brace her back successfully, the rider needs to think of keeping length in the torso, widening her own back and using her seat to encourage the horse forward to her hand. If "bracing" is overdone, the upper body moves backward behind the vertical, with the result that the horse is driven onto his forehand. If riders try too hard and *misuse* their backs, this can cause weakness that makes them vulnerable to injury. The Alexander Technique teaches correct *use* of the whole of the back, which guards against these injuries. The use of the back can be delicate but very powerful — there still has to be the correct interplay of leg, seat, and hand aids (figure 4.7). Good coordination and sensitivity to timing can be assisted by BodySense.

Understanding How the Spine is Structured
Riders tend to think their spines should be absolutely straight, but in fact, if viewed from the side the spine has a series of curves, which increases its shock absorbency and strength (figure 4.8). The spinous processes that are situated on the back of each vertebral body help to protect the spinal cord (figure 4.9). Weight is born by the main body of the vertebrae, which are situated approximately three inches in front of the spinous processes. This is crucial information as it affects the way you will use the spine to influence the horse's movement. Riders who mistakenly think that the weight bearing area is toward the back of the spinous processes will be inclined to sit behind the vertical. If you think of the spine as placed in the middle of the body, it will help change the distribution of weight over your seat bones.

Learning how to synchronise the action of the back and seat with the legs and hands is essential to the effectiveness of any aid. It is particularly important in lateral work, where the change of weight through the seat bones and the balance of the upper body is crucial. A horse cannot gain his full potential unless the rider has learned to use her back with varying degrees of subtlety according to the horse's standard of education and conformation.

Transitions

Intricate knowledge of the use of the spine is a great advantage during transitions. To execute good transitions, the rider must not disturb the horse's balance, yet many riders allow themselves to tip forward and therefore cannot synchronise with the movement of the horse's back. This promotes stiffness and causes the horse to fall on his forehand.

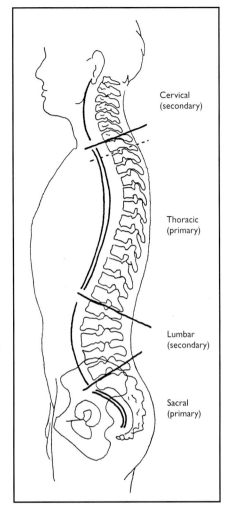

Figure 4.8 The curves of the spinal column viewed from the side.

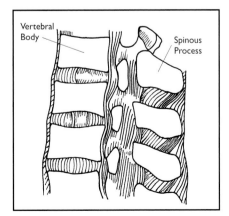

Figure 4.9 Cross section of the vertebral body viewed from the side. It is approximately three inches wide.

On the other hand, a rider who tips backward at the moment of a change in pace causes the horse to hollow and tighten his back and lift his head disturbing the balance of the *primary control*. In my BodySense courses I have found that in the transition from walk to halt riders learn how the hips and seat bones are moved as the horse steps into the transition.

If the rider stops the movement of her hips and lower back, this immobility blocks the movement through her horse's back and the horse responds by stopping. Riders are amazed at how little effort this takes, even with no rein contact! The same technique can also be applied in downward transitions from trot and canter, although a degree of subtlety and precision is needed for the seat bones to follow the new pace.

If you remain balanced during all transitions, then the steps that follow will obviously be easier for the horse. This is important because transitions are the key to achieving good, quality paces. If you think of the connection between your head, neck, and back (*primary control*) during a transition you will find it much easier to maintain this essential balance. Riders who try to hurry transitions by reacting too quickly and using excessive force cause loss of rhythm and balance, thus hampering the horse's progress.

Transitions from trot to canter can be difficult. One problem may be rigidity in the rider's spine in the sitting trot, which causes loss of balance and poise. In addition, aids may be clumsy because the rider is gripping with her legs. The goal is to keep the hip joints, pelvis, and back sufficiently free to follow the movement as the horse's spine rises into the canter. During canter strike-offs, try to think of allowing the horse's shoulders to come up in front of you. This will help to counteract the tendency to lurch forward.

With much time and practice you will acquire sufficient elasticity in the lower back to absorb all of your horse's movement. Alexander lessons help riders to experience different changes in texture throughout the length of the spine, but without lessons the experience of using the back in such an intricate manner is largely unobtainable to the majority of riders.

Training the Horse as You Train Yourself

The correct training of a horse bears certain parallels with the principles of the Alexander Technique for humans. The attributes we look for in a well-schooled horse could equally as well apply to his rider, and the "hands on" guidance of an Alexander teacher could be compared to the rider's appropriate aids to the horse.

In the training of the horse, the relationship between the horse's head, neck, and back is an essential indication of his overall balance, coordination, and quality of movement. Inexperienced trainers and riders can become too preoccupied with obtaining a specific position of the horse's head and neck. This excludes the vital role played by the back and focuses on positioning one part of the body without recognizing the need to work the horse as a whole. "These three main parts of the horse — neck, trunk, and hindlimbs are capable of independent reflex actions, which can be synchronised, provided that their freedom of movement is not impaired. If any one of these parts is prevented from functioning freely the whole mechanism of movement is disturbed" from *The Way to Perfect Horsemanship* by Udo Bürger.[20] Good trainers in all equestrian disciplines look for and encourage elasticity

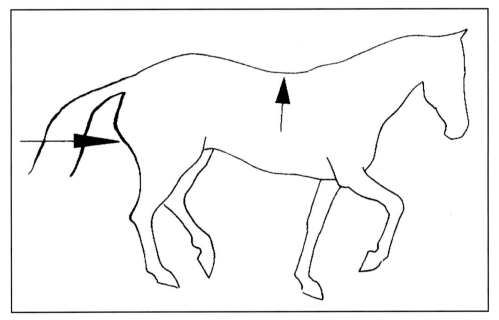

Figure 4.10 A horse is truly engaged when the activity from the hindquarters can travel through his back, neck, and head to his mouth.

through the horse's back, which depends on a release through the neck and on engagement from the hindquarters. A horse is only truly engaged and balanced when the activity from the hindquarters can travel through his back, neck, and head to his mouth (figure 4.10). The rider then picks up this forward energy with rein contact and it is as if the horse is stepping into the rider's hands from his hindquarters. The horse is then said to be "on the bit," working with the correct head–neck–back relationship (*primary control*). The goal of the Alexander

Technique and BodySense lessons is for riders also to work on their own head–neck–back relationship.

Stiffness in the poll and jaw will interfere with the freedom and swing of the horse's back, thereby affecting his overall balance and coordination of movement. A similar problem occurs if the rider is tight in the *atlanto-occipital joint* (comparable to the poll in the horse) or clenches the jaw. This could well make the difference between sitting to the trot with a soft back or bumping uncomfortably with a rigid spine. A rider who pulls her chin in and over-rounds the back could be compared to a horse that is "over-bent." The spine would be over-compressed and therefore lack elasticity. A rider jutting her chin out and hollowing her back would be similar to a horse "above the bit": the muscles in the back of the neck contract, causing an exaggerated curve in the spine so that the rider's legs are behind her body and she is tight and out of balance. In the horse, the hindquarters would be unable to propel him freely forward when he was above the bit.

Horses and humans are both vertebrates. Neither should be crooked through the spine. The horse is ridden forward from the leg to the hand to straighten him, and with "hands on" guidance from an Alexander teacher, the rider can be encouraged to release the neck, allowing the head to go forward and up, lengthening and widening the torso. If either horse or rider is stiff on either side of the neck, spine, pelvis, or through the ribs, straightness or alignment, and suppleness is restricted.

In dressage training, the changing relationship of the horse's head, neck, and back is shown through his outline. At training or novice level the horse carries approximately two-thirds of his body weight over the forehand and only one-third over his hindquarters. The aim at the training level or the novice stage is to teach the horse to step further underneath his body with his hind legs, so that he can use his neck and back to balance and accommodate the rider's additional weight. At more advanced levels, the horse is capable of stepping even further underneath his body and is therefore able to execute all movements with even greater impulsion, lightness, and cadence. More of the horse's body weight will be distributed over the hindquarters, which in turn increases the elasticity of the back and the suppleness of the limbs. This makes it easier for the horse to perform more advanced movements in lightness and enables the rider to sit correctly (figures 4.11–4.13).

Dressage training involves much more than changing an outline. Let's look again at the parallel with Alexander Technique lessons. Alexander teachers are working with subtleties that involve directing the mind and body to be used constructively, and horse trainers often

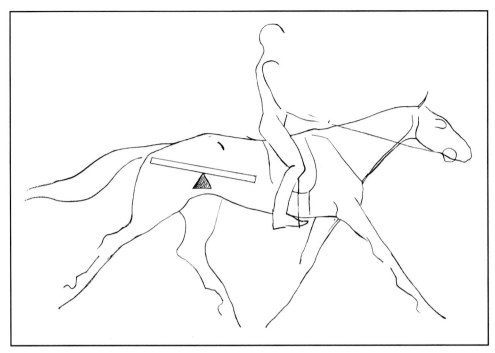

Figure 4.11 This horse is long in outline and there is more weight on the forehand. Tension in the jaw is evident by the angle of the horse's head.

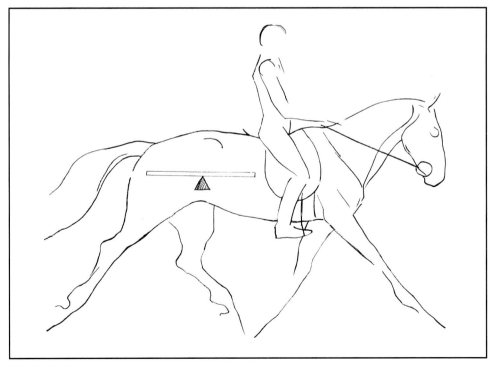

Figure 4.12 Here the hindquarters are beginning to engage more, which has lightened the shoulders and lessened the weight over the forelegs. There is increased suppleness in the neck and jaw.

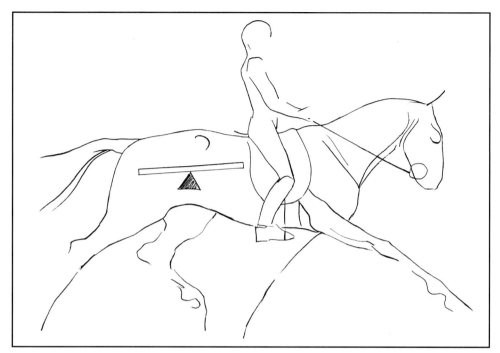

Figure 4.13 Now the horse has his back more engaged. His hocks are flexing to a greater degree, which means his hind legs can step further underneath his body. There is a greater impression of power coming from behind as the angle of the pelvis has changed, affecting the surrounding muscles.

refer to the way a horse uses himself. In the physical sense *"good use"* means that there is a good head–neck–back relationship and balance and movement is achieved with minimal muscular effort and lack of force. But this condition in the horse also requires the animal to have *good use* on a thinking and emotional level. The definition is as appropriate to horses as it is to humans! Unfortunately, both humans and horses too easily develop habitual responses that impede the proper functioning of the *primary control*.

I have already spoken about *"inhibition"* and its comparison to the half-halt. By inhibiting herself, the rider allows time to think, prepare, and re-balance. The rider imposes *inhibition* on the horse by means of the half-halt and through the aids — giving him time to quiet his mind and re-balance his body. It is the job of the rider to recognise and intercept the habitual responses in the horse, just as the Alexander teacher should also be aware of them in his pupil and guide her accordingly.

5

BodySense Techniques to Use During Competition

Thinking Affects Activity

We have seen how *habits* can affect our riding and our daily lives. Thoughts and mental attitudes also can have a profound effect on your body and how it performs at horse shows and events. Imagine the following scenario:

"Phew!" You breathe a sigh of relief as you land safely after the coffin fence. Everything is going smoothly as you prepare for the water jump. Then you remember that your horse dislikes water. You attempt to dispel any doubt, but your mind races back to all the occasions when your horse has refused to jump water. Before you know it, the inevitable has happened and your dream of a clear round has been shattered (figure 5.1).

Let's take a look at what has happened in this situation. The moment you start to think your body begins to react to those thoughts. The brain cannot distinguish between a positive thought and a negative one, it only acts to carry out the thought. Any thought produces an almost instant reaction in the body, which will also affect the horse. As Alexander observed, "you translate everything, whether physical, mental, or spiritual, into muscular tension."[21]

A Calm and Positive Frame of Mind

If you are in a negative frame of mind and mentally rehearse your horse stopping at the water, shying at the judges, or misbehaving, this is usually what you'll get. Being too desperate or trying too hard to get

Figure 5.1 What? Water – you must be joking!

it right ensures that riders become tense and produce undesired results. The Alexander Technique can be used to overcome these bad
habits, through *inhibition,* and to remain calm and self-confident through
proper breathing and *use* of self. Try some *"whispered ahs"* (see Chapter
Three, page 47) on the way to the competition. Make sure you allow
yourself plenty of time for preparation and that you keep yourself
calm and unstressed, not just on the morning of the competition but
during the week before as well. Learn to notice what aggravates your
nerves and take the time to plan your activities, so that they cause you
the least possible amount of stress.

Observing your voice and the quickness of your reaction can
help monitor anxiety. When your voice sounds high and sharp, you'll
know that your stress level is up. Ask your friends and family to tell
you how you sound, if you don't hear it yourself.

To discover the way in which your thoughts can influence your
body, you can perform the following experiments with the help of a
friend.

One of you will be person "A" and one will be person "B." "A"
directs her thoughts to her own head, while "B" gently pushes on
"A"'s sternum to find out how stable "A"'s body is (figure 5.2).

"B" then asks "A" to continue thinking of her head, and then to
direct her thoughts through the body to the feet. When "A" is ready,

"B" again pushes gently, using approximately the same force as before. This time is there any difference in "A"'s stability?

The aim of the experiment is to see whether the stability of the body changes according to the focus of the thought process. The conclusion we would expect is that the body is more stable when the mind is directed right down to the feet.

Now exchange roles and perform the experiment again, to see if the results are similar. This experiment should help you to experience how your attention can be directed to different parts of your body and what effect this has. The way you think and your mental attitude form the first steps toward gaining balance, suppleness, and strength.

For another experiment, stand facing each other. "A" asks "B" to hold an arm out to the side. "B" must then resist as "A" presses down on the forearm just above "B"'s wrist (figure 5.3). Notice the amount of resistance. Lower the arm.

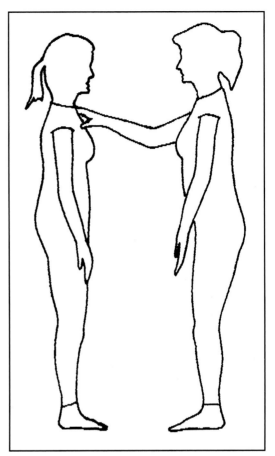

Figure 5.2 Note the position of the sternum on the body. Many riders are unaware that tension here affects the way they hold the reins, which often hampers the horse's movement.

"A" then asks "B" to think of her body as an oak tree with the torso as the trunk and the outstretched arm as a strong branch that is growing from that trunk. "A" then presses down on "B"'s arm and notices how much pressure is needed to move the arm. Was the amount of pressure different from the first time? When you were the oak tree did you feel able to resist more easily?

Exchange roles again and see if you get similar results.

This experiment once again shows the power of thought and how it can affect the body if you learn to use your thinking in a positive way. Successful riders have found ways of eliminating negative past experiences and thought patterns. No one is superhuman, and even these riders have had their fair share of difficult horses and falls. However, they have learned to use their minds constructively rather than destructively.

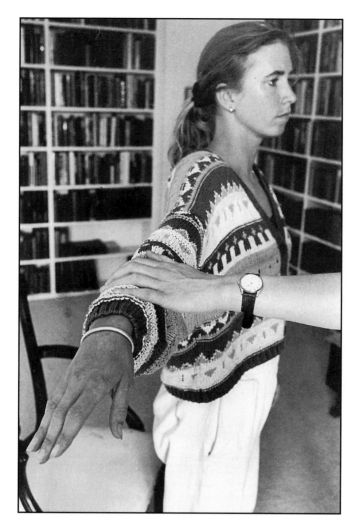

Figure 5.3
Testing resistance.

How Your Physical and Mental Condition Affects Poise in Performance

"The Alexander Technique teaches us how to enhance and utilise all the qualities needed to acquire and develop poise."
Daniel Pevsner, Fellow of the British Horse Society (FBHS)[22]

What makes a talented rider stand out from the crowd? Is it ostentatious movement of her body that draws your eye, or is it the quietness and grace of her riding technique that transfixes you?

Riders who tend to attract our attention make riding look elegant and effortless. There is no excessive movement. Horse and rider blend together and exude that special quality known as "poise." The *Oxford English Dictionary* defines poise as "composure," or "dignity of manner," "balanced and prepared for action" — something every rider needs whether they are competing or not.

How Tension Affects Poise

Actors spend many years learning how to remain poised despite the stresses of performing on stage. Riders need to be poised as much as actors, although many of them do not know how to achieve this. Instead, they become so obsessed with their horse's way of going that they forget just how much their own bodies can influence the horse's freedom of movement. Too much anxiety while performing can severely limit a rider's chances of obtaining poise. It causes riders to use their brains in a way that hinders their ability to achieve their true potential. As you learned in Chapter Three, it is the beta brain waves associated with "hard eyes" that may spoil a performance. The slower alpha waves associated with "soft eyes" will help to quicken the mind, but they are only produced when the rider is calm. *Inhibition*, as discussed in Chapter Two, can also help control your reactions successfully and encourage greater awareness and calmness.

Preparing for an Event

A fit horse needs a fit rider. Even though professional riders spend countless hours in the saddle, they recognise the need to participate in other sporting activities to improve their physical condition, especially if they are competing in combined training or endurance events. However, it is not the quantity of exercise that is important, but the quality of your training. During BodySense courses we encourage appropriate effort (*good use*) for maximum efficiency, thereby reducing the risk of exhaustion and injury.

Interval training has been used for increasing fitness in various sports for people as well as horses. Before it was invented, riders would trot, canter, and gallop their horses for miles to build up fitness. Unfortunately, a great many horses experienced lameness from overwork in the process. Michael Dickenson, now a successful racehorse trainer in the United States, was probably the first to make a scientific study of interval training in England in the 1970s, with the result that he trained the first five horses to finish in the 1983 Cheltenham Gold Cup race, an achievement that had never been matched before and may never be equaled.

During interval training an athlete — either horse or human — will stress their heart, lungs, and muscles, rest a short while to partially recover, and then exercise to a stressed point again. In both the horse and human, the respiratory and circulatory systems are strengthened and stress tolerance is increased. This can be monitored carefully by checking pulse rates. The most significant factor is the speed with which the pulse, and therefore respiration, returns to normal. The athlete (either horse or human) is allowed to partially recover so that he never reaches a point of fatigue where the body is more susceptible to injury. Although it is important to take care of the heart and lungs, it is no good developing them at the expense of the rest of the body.

Balance of horse and rider (see Chapter Three, page 51) is crucial to overall fitness, since it will determine whether they can move easily across uneven terrain without strain or damage. Many exercise routines focus too much on working particular areas of the body to the detriment of overall coordination. Too often people exercise for one hour a day and forget about how they are using their bodies for the rest of the day. "Chronic posture imbalances bend and stretch our bodies in unhealthy ways. Skeletal and muscular symmetry is distorted. Circulation may be impaired. Joints and bones bear added pressures. Tension pools in muscles that must constantly strain against gravity to maintain us upright. After a while, we begin to note small crookednesses. Instead of true balance, we are held in a complicated array of offsetting compensations."[23]

6

Enjoying Your Riding

What makes you want to ride? Many people never stop to wonder why they actually enjoy riding horses. The horse represents different things to different people. For some, the horse's beauty and elegance offer an opportunity to practice and enjoy the classical art of equitation, while for others the speed and excitement of racing can be exhilarating. For some the horse is a means of competing in a sport such as combined training or endurance riding. Other riders find that the horse provides an escape into the country and the fresh air (figure 6.1).

Disabled riders cherish the rapport they establish with an animal who gives them mobility, trust, and who will not be judgmental. Horses and ponies can instill great confidence and many will look after their riders when it really matters.

Finding an affinity with an animal that is strong, powerful and yet highly sensitive is a privilege sought after and cherished by most riders. People who swim with wild dolphins say it is the only way to experience unconditional love, but horses show similar qualities to the dolphin in the generosity of their nature. After all, it is only because of their kindness that horses allow us to sit on their backs! There is no doubt that horses are our teachers as in the title of Alois Podhajsky's book, *My Horses, My Teachers*.[24] They can act as a medium for gaining a clearer understanding of ourselves. An unspoiled horse is a reflection of the rider's clarity of thought and understanding of the goals to be achieved and the correct means of gaining them. Focusing on positive, obtainable progress and treating the horse with the respect it deserves is an attitude all riders should cultivate. What a rider is thinking about during a lesson can enhance or destroy her enjoyment, expand or limit her true potential, and create joy of learning or learning blocks (figure 6.2).

Figure 6.1 People ride for all sorts of reasons. Sidesaddle is enjoying a revival even among the younger members of the family.

Figure 6.2 If you carry the weight of the world on your shoulders it will spoil your lesson.

"I must get it right today." "I expect she (the instructor) thinks I'm wasting her time." "I'll never be good enough." Riders often become negative because they are set on reaching a goal. If for example, a horse has difficulty maintaining the length of step in extended trot for eight strides or more, but has managed three, it is so easy to obliterate those three lovely strides because you are so focused on obtaining ten. Be happy with the three and feel that you have a foundation to build on. Having expectations that are unrealistic can also reduce learning. Even worse, the brain gets into a habit of sabotaging any improvement, no matter how significant, just because the result has not matched the desire.

The importance of goal setting, however, should not be devalued. Realistic goals should be planned and matched to horse and rider. For instance, when teaching a horse to jump, a trotting pole and then a small cross pole are used before a higher fence is incorporated. Also, the horse should be suitable for the task at hand. Don't expect a Thoroughbred to pull a plow or a Shire horse to go racing. However, this doesn't mean to say that every rider cannot improve within the capabilities of herself and her horse. Everyone should have the chance to enjoy the experience of gaining greater wisdom. The horse is a partner, not a servant; without his cooperation a rider can satisfy none of her riding ambitions. These facts very much embrace the philosophy

Figure 6.3 See how your horse moves when free...

of my teaching. In the words of Franz Mairinger, former Chief Rider of the Spanish Riding School, "If you want to know how a horse should be ridden, see how he moves by himself when free. How he walks, trots and canters…Have a close look and see the beauty, the rhythm and harmony of his movements. Then sit down, close your eyes and try to burn this picture of effortless grace, beauty and harmony deep into your mind, your heart. Never forget it. Because it is the way you should ride your horse"[25] (figure 6.3).

Epilogue

Can I Learn the Alexander Technique Without a Teacher?

It is not practical to assume that you can learn the Alexander Technique without a teacher. F.M. Alexander took more than seven years to devise the method, and skilled teachers must use their hands and their words to communicate the Technique in order for it to be fully understood. I would strongly recommend that you find a fully trained teacher to give you guidance.

Finding an Alexander Teacher

There are two major professional societies: the British-based Society of Teachers of the Alexander Technique (STAT) and the North American Society of Teachers of the Alexander Technique (NASTAT). To be recognised by a society, an Alexander teacher must have attended a three-year full-time training course affiliated to a society. This means that the training course must be run by a Director who has a minimum of seven years teaching experience, and an assistant with at least five years teaching experience. The student-teacher ratio during each training course should be at least five students to one teacher. Classes are small, usually no more than fifteen to twenty students in all, as this gives everyone the opportunity for individual attention. Each society supplies a complete list of qualified teachers. The best way to find your nearest teacher is to contact the society in your area.

If there is no teacher available in your area, you may consider attending a residential course. These usually take place over three to five days and are an ideal way of getting started. It's amazing how much a group of like-minded people can inspire one another and learn from observing each other. Another way to arrange some lessons is to ask a teacher to come to you. If you can organise eight to ten people for a concentrated short course of individual lessons, this is a good way to learn and is preferable for pupils with pressured work commitments. As mentioned previously, an Alexander Technique teacher doesn't need to be a rider to teach you the fundamentals of the Technique; once you've learned these you may want to find a teacher who is a riding specialist, but it certainly isn't necessary when starting lessons.

GLOSSARY

Atlanto-Occipital Joint
See figure 1.7, page 7.

Direction
The sending of messages from the brain to the body to prevent misuse.

Endgaining
An overemphasis on achieving a given end or goal, which distracts attention from the appropriate steps or means whereby needed to achieve the end. Endgaining prevents the application of inhibition and direction and therefore interferes with the functioning of the primary control.

Good Use
A well-balanced head–neck–back relationship (primary control) when all parts of the psychophysical organism are working well together simultaneously.

Habit
An acquired way of responding that becomes familiar, comfortable and beneath the levels of consciousness and therefore automatic.

Inhibition
The ability to consciously "drive a wedge" between stimulus and response. It is the first vital step to changing a habit and allowing the primary control to function freely.

Kinesthetic (Awareness)
This term describes the sensations from the body that register tension, quality, and speed of movement and spacial awareness. It is often referred to as the lost sixth sense.

Means Whereby
Focusing on the steps involved in reaching a goal.

Misuse
An excessive degree of muscular tension and effort orginating from the malfunctioning of the primary control.

Primary Control
The dynamic relationship between the head, neck, and back that governs the rest of the body balance and coordination.

Sense of Feel
A rider's ability to feel in detail what is happening to her own body and that of her horse's.

Sensory Appreciation
Describes how our perception of ourselves and our environment is governed by what feels familiar and right — our habits. When we change our habits, our perceptions change, often making us feel uneasy.

Use
Alexander borrowed this term from the horse world. He expanded its meaning to include the total pattern of behaviour at any the precise moment. He emphasised that by use he meant the use of all parts of the psycho-physical organism working together.

Whispered Ah
A breathing exercise that helps focus attention on breathing while enhancing relaxation, see Chapter Three.

PHOTOGRAPH AND ILLUSTRATION
CREDITS

Photos

Christopher Smart
Pages 2, 4–6, 8–11, 17, 24, 25, 32, 33, 37, 39–43, 46, 50, 53, 55, 59, 73 (figure 4.5), 84

Mary Scott
Page 14

Noel Harrison
Page 21

Colin and Julia Tully
Page 20

C.J. Taylor
Page 56

P. Harding
Page 58

J. Benger and Isabel Haskett
Page 88

Daniel Pevsner
Pages 69, 73 (figure 4.6)

Bob Langrish
Page 89

Line drawings

Sebastian Rice-Edwards
Pages 26, 31, 33, 36, 38, 45, 46, 48, 57, 60 (figure 3.38), 71, 74, 77, 83

David Gorman
Pages 7, 16, 17, 30, 31, 34, 35, 51, 52, 54, 60 (figure 3.37), 75

Alex Newcombe
Pages 62, 63

Jo Taylor
Pages 79, 80

Cartoons

Jan Farnes
Pages 68, 82, 88

ALEXANDER TECHNIQUE PROFESSIONAL SOCIETIES

The following societies will provide a list of teachers of the Alexander Technique who have completed the three years of an approved training course (please send a stamped, self-addressed envelope).

Australia
Australian Society of Teachers of the Alexander Technique (AUSTAT)
PO Box 716
Darlinghurst
Sydney
NSW 2010

Brazil
Associação Brasileira da Técnica Alexander (ABTA)
Caixa Postal 16020
Rio de Janeiro
22220-970

Canada
Canadian Society of Teachers of the Alexander Technique (CANSTAT)
1472 East St. Joseph Blvd.
Apt. #4
Montreal
Quebec H2J IM5

Denmark
Danish Society of Teachers of the Alexander Technique (DFLAT)
v/ Marc Grue, Secretary
Amager Faelledvej 4
DK-2300 Copenhagen S

France
Association Française des Professional Technique Alexander (APTA)
42, Terrasse de l'Iris
La Défense 2
92400 Coubevoie

Germany
German Society of Teachers of the Alexander Technique (GLAT)
Postfach 5312
79020 Frieburg

Israel
Israeli Society of Teachers of the Alexander Technique (ISTAT)
PO Box 715
Karkur 37106

The Netherlands
Netherlands Society of Teachers of the Alexander Technique
Postbus 15591
1001 NB
Amsterdam

South Africa
South African Society of Teachers of the Alexander Technique (SASTAT)
5 Leinster Rd.
Green Point 8001

Switzerland
Swiss Society of Teachers of the Alexander Technique (SVLAT)
Postfach
CH-8032
Zürich

United Kingdom
The Society of Teachers of the Alexander Technique (STAT)
20 London House
266 Fulham Road
London SW10 9EL
e-mail: stat@pavilion.co.uk

United States of America
North American Society of Teachers of the Alexander Technique (NASTAT)
3010 Hennepin Ave., South
Suite 10
Minneapolis, Minnesota 55408
e-mail: nastat@ix.netcom.com

NOTES

1 Udo Bürger, *The Way to Perfect Horsemanship.* (London: J.A. Allen, 1986).

2 Edward Maisel, *The Resurrection of the Body*, (Boston & London, Shambhala, 1969). Notes of instruction from students of F.M. Alexander.

3 F.M. Alexander, *The Use of the Self,* (Long Beach, California: Centerline Press, 1984).

4 F.M. Alexander, *Man's Supreme Inheritance,* (Long Beach, California: Centerline Press, 1986).

5 Nuno Oliveira. *Reflections on Equestrian Art*, London: J.A. Allen, 1990.

6 F.M. Alexander, *The Use of the Self,* (Long Beach, California: Centerline Press,. 1984).

7 Edward Maisel, *The Resurrection of the Body*, (Boston & London, Shambhala, 1969).

8 Bill and Barbara Conable, *How to Learn the Alexander Technique*, (Columbus, Ohio: Andover Road Press, 1991).

9 Udo Bürger, *The Way to Perfect Horsemanship* (London: J.A. Allen, 1986).

10 Sally Swift, *Centered Riding* (North Pomfret, Vermont: Trafalgar Square Publishing, 1985).

11 Sally Swift, *Centered Riding* (North Pomfret, Vermont: Trafalgar Square Publishing, 1985).

12 Jean Licart, *Basic Equitation* (New York: Arco, 1972).

13 Wilhelm Müseler, *Riding Logic* (New York: Simon & Schuster, 1987).

14 Udo Bürger, *The Way to Perfect Horsemanship* (London: J.A. Allen, 1986).

15 F.M. Alexander, *Constructive Conscious Control of the Individual* (London: Methuen, 1923).

16 Alois Podhajsky, *Complete Training of Horse and Rider* (North Hollywood, California: Wilshire Books, 1982).

17 Nuno Oliveira. *Reflections on Equestrian Art*, London: J.A. Allen, 1990.

18 Alois Podhajsky, *Complete Training of Horse and Rider* (North Hollywood, California: Wilshire Books, 1982).

19 Daniel Pevsner, "Equitation and the Alexander Technique" (a lecture presented to Alexander teachers at Letchmore Farm, Herefordshire, England, April 10, 1994).

20 Udo Bürger, *The Way to Perfect Horsemanship* (London: J.A. Allen, 1986).

21 Edward Maisel, *The Resurrection of the Body*, (Boston & London, Shambhala, 1969).

22 Sylvia Loch, "Trainers of Our Time," *Horse and Rider* (UK), January 1986.

23 Robert Rickover, *Fitness Without Stress* (Portland, Oregon: Metamorphous Press, 1988).

24 Alois Podhajsky, *My Horses, My Teachers* (North Pomfret, Vermont: Trafalgar Square Publishing, 1997).

25 Franz Mairinger, *Horses are Made to be Horses* (New York: Howell Book House, 1986).

RECOMMENDED RESOURCES

On Riding

Bürger, Udo. *The Way to Perfect Horsemanship.* North Pomfret, Vermont: Trafalgar Square Publishing, 1998 (US). London: J.A. Allen, 1986 (UK).

Hölzel, Petra and Wolfgang, and Martin Plewa. *Dressage Tips and Training Solutions: Using the German Training System.* North Pomfret, Vermont: Trafalgar Square Publishing, 1995 (US). Addington: Kenilworth Press, 1995 (UK).

Kyrklund, Kyra and Jytte Lemkow. *Dressage With Kyra: The Kyra Kyrklund Training Method.* North Pomfret, Vermont: Trafalgar Square Publishing, 1998 (US). Addington: Kenilworth Press, 1998 (UK).

Loch, Sylvia. *The Classical Rider: Being At One with Your Horse.* North Pomfret, Vermont: Trafalgar Square Publishing, 1997 (US). London: J.A. Allen & Co., 1997 (UK).

Savoie, Jane. *That Winning Feeling!: Program Your Mind for Peak Performance.* North Pomfret, Vermont: Trafalgar Square Publishing, 1992 (US). London: J.A. Allen & Co., 1992 (UK).

Savoie, Jane. *Cross-Train Your Horse: Simple Dressage for Every Horse, Every Sport.* North Pomfret, Vermont: Trafalgar Square Publishing, 1998 (US). London: J.A. Allen & Co., 1998 (UK).

Savoie, Jane. *More Cross-Training: Build a Better Performance Horse with Dressage.* North Pomfret, Vermont: Trafalgar Square Publishing, 1998 (US). London: J.A. Allen & Co., 1998 (UK).

Swift, Sally, *Centered Riding.* North Pomfret, Vermont: Trafalgar Square Publishing, 1985 (US). London: Random House UK, 1998 (UK).

On the Alexander Technique

Alexander, F.M. *The Use of the Self.* Long Beach, California: Centerline Press, 1984.

Barlow, Wilfred. *The Alexander Principle.* Rochester, Vermont: Inner Traditions, 1991.

Drake, Jonathan. *Thorson's Introductory Guide to the Alexander Technique.* San Francisco: HarperCollins, 1993.

Gelb, Michael. *Body Learning: An Introduction to the Alexander Technique.* New York: Henry Holt & Co., 1996.

Gray, John. *The Alexander Technique: A Complete Course in How to Hold and Use Your Body for Maximum Energy.* New York: St. Martin's Press, 1991.

Leibowitz, Judith and Bill Connington. *The Alexander Technique.* New York: HarperCollins, 1991.

Park, Glen. *The Art of Changing: A New Approach to the Alexander Technique.* England: Ashgrove Press, 1997.

Stevens, Chris. *Alexander Technique.* Boston: Charles E. Tuttle Co., 1994.

Alexander books are available from The Society of Teachers of the Alexander Technique (STAT) and North American Society of Teachers of the Alexander Technique (NASTAT). See the list of Alexander Technique societies on page 95-96.

On BodySense

For information on BodySense courses and an audiotape by Sally Tottle, contact:

S. A. Tottle
Monmouth Natural Health Centre
Cippenham House
Monmouthshire
United Kingdom
Web site: http://www.bodysense.i2g.com

INDEX